Forestry Commission
Handbook 5

Urban Forestry Practice

Edited by B.G. Hibberd
Research Communications Officer,
Forestry Commission

Prepared in co-operation with the
Department of the Environment

LONDON: HER MAJESTY'S STATIONERY OFFICE

HMSO BOOKS

HMSO publications are available from:

HMSO Publications Centre
(Mail and telephone orders only)
PO Box 276, London, SW8 5DT
Telephone orders 01-873 9090
General enquiries 01-873 0011
(queuing system in operation for both numbers)

HMSO Bookshops
49 High Holborn, London, WC1V 6HB   01-873 0011 (Counter service only)
258 Broad Street, Birmingham, B1 2HE   021-643 3740
Southey House, 33 Wine Street, Bristol, BS1 2BQ   (0272) 264306
9–21 Princess Street, Manchester, M60 8AS   061-834 7201
80 Chichester Street, Belfast, BT1 4JY   (0232) 238451
71 Lothian Road, Edinburgh, EH3 9AZ   031-228 4181

HMSO's Accredited Agents
(see Yellow Pages)
and through good booksellers

ISBN 0 11 710273 3

ODC 26 : 913 : (410)

Keywords: Urban forestry

Acknowledgements

Much of the advice and information in this Handbook dealing with the establishment and health of urban trees comes directly from research funded by the Department of the Environment. The Department has also encouraged and assisted the production of this Handbook from the outset. In particular, thanks are due to John Peters and Graham Davis who have given invaluable guidance as referees.

The Countryside Commission and Forestry Commission are partners in the promotion and development of urban forestry and Rick Minter of the Countryside Commission's Conservation Branch is at the forefront of this co-operation. His work as referee and advisor for this Handbook is gratefully acknowledged.

Drs Dick Morris and Steven Newman of the Open University together with Chris Rose of the Milton Keynes Development Corporation have offered sound guidance at all stages of the Handbook's development. Within the Forestry Commission thanks are due to Alistair Scott for his co-ordination of responses from other senior staff and his work as referee.

Special mention should be made of authors from outside of the Forestry Commission. Without their contributions this Handbook could never have been sufficiently comprehensive to do justice to the breadth of the subject.

Finally, the editor wishes to record his gratitude for the timely and careful work done in the Typing Pool at the Forest Research Station, Alice Holt Lodge.

Front cover

Top   Urban landscape with mature trees; Morpeth, Northumberland. (38333)

Bottom   Tree planting in Surrey with David Bellamy. (38738)
City centre planting; Newcastle-upon-Tyne. (38381)
Harvesting quality timber generates income; Leeds City Council. (T. Exley)

Back cover
The Forestry Commission's Chopwell Wood in Tyne and Wear has served the needs of an industrial urban population for many decades.

Contents

Foreword

Most town dwellers are countrymen at heart, and trees in built-up areas satisfy a deeply-felt need. It is easy, however, to take trees for granted, something which was demonstrated to us so dramatically by the tragic loss of many fine urban trees in south-east England during the great storm of October 1987. The storm also vividly brought home to us the fact that trees can be retained too long beyond their prime and that careful planning is needed to maintain a continuing tree cover.

I therefore warmly welcome this Forestry Commission Handbook which gives practical advice on how to establish trees, especially on difficult sites, and how to manage them for a variety of purposes. Its publication is designed as part of a major initiative by the Countryside Commission and the Forestry Commission to promote forestry for the community. Much of the Forestry Commission research work on which the Handbook is based has been funded by the Department of the Environment.

The need for such a Handbook was identified at the first UK Conference on urban forestry held at Wolverhampton in the spring of 1988. The Conference brought together delegates from this country and from overseas with a wide range of interests and experience, and with a common concern to do more about growing and managing trees near where most people live. The outcome has been a fresh enthusiasm for using trees, in all their variety, to improve the quality of life in and near our towns and cities.

I commend this Handbook to all who are concerned with the quality of our urban environment.

John MacGregor

The Rt Hon John MacGregor OBE, MP
Minister of Agriculture, Fisheries and Food

Summary

Practical advice is provided on the establishment and subsequent management of trees and woodlands in urban and urban fringe areas of the United Kingdom. The Handbook draws heavily on the research work funded by the Department of the Environment and carried out at the Forestry Commission's Research Station at Alice Holt in Surrey, England. The history and development of urban forestry in Britain and the aims of tree planting in and around towns are outlined. Public involvement and the planning and management of community events and projects are described. A section devoted to preparation and planting deals with site preparation, choice of species, choice of planting stock and establishment and early maintenance operations. A further section deals with aftercare and management including pruning practice, diseased and damaged trees, buildings and trees, and the management of existing woodlands. Possibilities for generating revenue from tree felling are described and discussed. Further information includes advice on the design and management of contracts, addresses for information advice and funding, and a comprehensive list of common diseases and disorders of trees. A bibliography is included.

Sommaire

On pourvoit des conseils pratiques sur l'établissement et la gestion ultérieure des arbres et des bois à l'intérieur et autour des zones urbaines dans Le Royaume-Uni. Le Manuel apporte beaucoup des recherches fondées par le Département de l'Environnement et performées par la Station d'Essai Forestière de la Commission Forestière à Alice Holt, Surrey, Angleterre. On esquisse l'histoire et le développement de la foresterie urbaine dans Le Royaume-Uni, et les buts de la plantation des arbres dans et autour des villes. On décrit la participation publique, et la planification et la gestion des fonctions et projets communautaires. Une partie consacrée à la preparation et la plantation traite de la préparation des stations, le choix des essences, le choix des plants, l'établissement, et les entretiens culturaux.

Une autre partie traite des entretiens ultérieurs et de la gestion, y compris l'ébranchage, les arbres malades et endommagés, les bâtiments et les arbres, et la gestion des bois actuels. On décrit et discute les possibilités qui existent d'engendrer des revenus par l'abattage des arbres. Les autres renseignements comprennent des conseils sur la préparation et la gestion des contrats, des adresses utiles pour l'information, le conseil et la provision des fonds, et une liste d'ensemble des maladies et des indispositions communes des arbres. Une bibliographie est y compris.

Zusammenfassung

Praktischer Rat wird über die Begründung und die spätere Bewirtschaftung von Bäumen und Wäldern in Stadtbezirken und Stadtrandgebieten in Grossbritannien gegeben. Das Handbuch nimmt stark in Anspruch die Forschungsarbeiten, die durch das Umweltministerium fundiert und in der Forschungsanstalt der Britischen Forstkommission in Alice Holt (Surrey) ausgeführt worden sind. Die Geschichte und die Entwicklung der städtischen Forstwirtschaft in Grossbritannien sowie die Ziele der Baumpflanzung in den Städten und in ihrer Nähe werden im Umriss dargestellt. Die Mitwirkung der Öffentlichkeit und die Planung und Leitung von Gemeinveranstaltungen und Projekten werden beschrieben. Ein Abschnitt behandelt Vorbereitung und Pflanzung, nämlich Standortvorbereitung, Baumartenwahl, Pflanzgutwahl, Pflanzenbegründung und frühe Pflegemassnahmen. Ein weiterer Abschnitt behandelt die spätere Pflege und Bewirtschaftung, einschliesslich Aufastung, kranke und beschädigte Bäume, Gebäude und Bäume, und die Bewirtschaftung der schon bestehenden Wälder. Die Möglichkeiten, die zur Verfügung stehen, um Einkommen von Baumfällung zu erzeugen, werden beschrieben und diskutiert. Weitere Informationen behandeln: die Abschliessung und Durchführung von Verträgen; Adressen für Auskunft, Rat und Fundierung; und eine umfangreiche Liste der gemeinen Baumkrankheiten. Eine Bibliographie wird auch eingeschlossen.

How to use this Handbook

Urban forestry practice has been designed to meet a wide variety of needs reflecting the many and varied disciplines and requirements involved in urban forestry. If each chapter is read in sequence a comprehensive picture will emerge, through planning to establishment and ultimately tree maturity and utilisation. Depending on the subject, some chapters deal mainly with principles and objectives, while others are more technical containing specifications and practical information. Many students and others newly involved in urban forestry may wish to read the Handbook as a text book, while many professionals and others concerned with day-to-day practice will wish to dip into the Handbook seeking out areas of their own interests. With the latter group of readers in mind, this Handbook has been divided into six sections each of which contains chapters dealing with a particular aspect of urban forestry.

Readers of *Urban forestry practice* who wish to extend their reading to include the traditional aims of woodland management, such as timber production, wildlife conservation or game, will find suitable additional information in the Forestry Commission's companion Handbooks, *Forestry practice* and *Farm woodland practice*.

Urban Forests

This section forms a general introduction to the Handbook and describes briefly the history and development of urban forestry in Britain. The aims of tree planting in and around towns are outlined.

1 The need for advice

Definition of urban forestry

The aim of this Handbook is to provide practical advice on the establishment and subsequent management of trees and woodlands in urban and urban fringe areas. The term urban forestry is applied to many different situations in a variety of countries; not surprisingly this has led to imprecise definition.

In Britain there are three main types of forestry. The first of these is forestry undertaken with the primary aim of producing timber; the plantations and woods concerned are often referred to as 'traditional forestry'. They are usually extensive and located in rural areas. The second category can be described as 'small woodlands' where timber production may still be an important consideration in management, although sometimes subservient to aims such as wildlife conservation, shelter, game management, recreation and landscape improvement. The third category – which we will call urban forestry – embraces trees grown in and close to urban areas for their value in the landscape, for recreation, and including trees in streets, avenues, urban parks, on land reclaimed from previous industrial use, as well as those in urban woodlands and gardens. The possibility of producing timber from these trees is not ruled out, although it is unlikely that this will be a primary aim.

Traditional forestry is usually managed by professional foresters working in large organisations to clearly defined objectives. Small woodlands are usually in private ownership and the landowners concerned (often farmers) will obtain advice according to their individual needs from consultants, voluntary bodies and the Forestry Commission. Urban forestry very often relies upon the close co-operation of the local authority, private owners (including industrial interests), voluntary groups and the local community. Where one exists, the Forestry Officer in the local authority occupies a key role in ensuring the success of urban forestry schemes; keen and knowledgeable individuals operating within the various voluntary bodies also contribute. But because of the wide variety of interests and aims involved, there is more danger of projects failing in urban forestry than in less specialised forms of forestry. This danger is enhanced if there is a lack of understanding of the basic technical rules for successful tree establishment or later maintenance.

Products and by-products

Wherever tree growing is a managed activity, outputs should be expected and planned for. Outputs can be tangible in terms of saleable timber for industry and this is the usual benefit gained from traditional forestry in Britain. Woodland can also be managed in order to preserve or improve the habitat for wildlife. Similarly, the provision of recreational facilities and the development of attractive woodland landscapes are outputs which should be sought in any tree management scheme.

In urban forestry some very special outputs become obtainable. For example, trees planted and cared for by the town school can have their product quite literally carried in the minds of children whose close involvement with trees will enhance and expand their understanding and appreciation of living things and their ecology.

Today there is a special need to attract new development into once derelict urban areas. The provision of green and pleasant working and living environments in our towns and cities is an important contribution in that effort. The use of trees in the creation of urban green space can enhance its value and eventually provide the basis for a financial benefit through the advent of new industrial investment, a gain which is quite as commercial as growing timber for industry.

Basic needs of trees

Whatever the objectives in planting and managing trees, whether in urban or rural areas, healthy growth can only be achieved if the biological needs of the tree are catered for. Many urban environments and reclaimed sites are hostile to tree

38391

PLATE 1
Scots pine woodland in Washington
New Town.

38354

PLATE 2
Jesmond Dene, Newcastle-upon-Tyne.

11

PLATE 3
City centre woodland, Edinburgh.

growth, sometimes because of pollution, but more often because of basic difficulties in ensuring that tree roots have an adequate supply of water and oxygen. It is essential to the success of urban forestry schemes that these basic needs are understood and that the appropriate choice of species, site treatment and subsequent management on each location are carefully related to the trees' needs and the nature of the site.

Urban forestry has a reputation for being much more expensive than forestry in rural Britain, especially at the critical stages of initial planting and early aftercare. Some high levels of expenditure may be unavoidable because of a small scale of operations and high costs of site preparation. But the advice contained in this Handbook describes cost-effective methods for tree establishment and management based on experience in research and the results applied to practice in the field. For example, in Chapter 7 the reader will find guidance on the use of small well balanced planting stock which will not only yield better results in terms of survival and fast early growth, but will also be a good deal cheaper to obtain than the more commonly used standards.

The role of trees in Britain

Britain's climate and soils suit a very wide range of temperate tree species and over most of the British Isles the natural climax vegetation in the absence of man and his browsing animals would be tree cover. Despite this, Britain is one of the least wooded countries in Europe (Table 1.1).

In 1919 when the Forestry Commission was set up to promote the neglected interests of forestry and trees, Britain had less than 5% woodland cover. Since then a huge effort has been made to increase the number of trees growing in Britain and today about 10% of the country is under woodlands. This is still far below the European average and as Britain is a huge net importer of wood and wood products the aim of most traditional forestry schemes has concentrated and continues to concentrate on timber production by means of plantation forestry.

From this viewpoint urban forestry may appear to occupy a position out of the mainstream of the forestry effort in this country. In terms of area and amount of wood produced urban forestry may seem almost insignificant. However, in terms of public use the potential for urban forestry appears limitless and there can be no doubt that urban forestry is the one category of

Table 1.1 Land use – international comparisons

Country	Total land area (million ha)	Percentage of total area		
		Forestry	Agriculture	Urban and other
Great Britain	**22.7**	**10**	**77**	**13**
United Kingdom	24.1	10	78	13
Belgium/Luxembourg	3.3	21	46	33
Denmark	4.2	12	67	21
France	54.6	27	57	16
West Germany	24.4	30	49	21
Greece	13.1	20	70	10
Ireland	6.9	5	83	12
Italy	29.4	22	59	20
Netherlands	3.4	9	60	32
Portugal	9.2	40	36	24
Spain	49.9	31	61	8
EEC Countries	**222.5**	**24**	**60**	**15**
Norway	30.8	27	3	70
Sweden	41.2	64	9	27
Finland	30.5	76	8	16
USA	916.7	29	47	24
Canada	922.1	35	8	56
USSR	2227.2	42	27	31
Japan	37.6	67	14	19
World	**13078.9**	**31**	**36**	**33**

Sources: GB and UK – CSO Annual Abstract of Statistics, 1988.   Elsewhere – FAO Production Yearbook Vol.40, 1986.
Notes: 1. Forestry areas include unproductive woodland.   2. Other land includes mountains, tundra, desert, etc.

forestry which can truly be described as being principally for people. Bearing this in mind the need for community involvement in tree planting schemes in and around urban areas must be seen as essential. Community involvement is also a major way of avoiding or at least reducing intentional damage such as vandalism and also unintentional damage due to ignorance about trees and their needs.

In many countries 'town forests' and similar woodlands owned and managed by local communities are commonplace (see Figure 1.1). This situation is rare in Britain and the co-operative effort between landowner, local authority, industrial interests, voluntary bodies and people living in the local community is something which requires a special effort to develop. Evidence of failure to achieve such co-operation can be seen in many towns and cities up and down the country.

The 'municipal tree' planted as part of an architectural design but without reference to the needs or interests of the local community needs to be seen as a thing of the past. Trees cannot be made vandal-proof. Unless the people who live with them perceive them as being part of their desired environment then trees will at best be ignored and perhaps damaged due to ignorance. At worst they will be wilfully destroyed.

Owing to the tremendous upsurge of interest in the environment there are probably more people today in Britain interested in trees and keen to plant and grow them than ever before. This, coupled with the urgent need to rehabilitate industrial areas in Britain, means that urban forestry has a new impetus. There is a tide of enthusiasm for trees in urban areas which has the potential quite literally to change the face of Britain's towns and cities. However, if it is to be sustained this enthusiasm must be fed with satisfying results. Far too often the enthusiasm of people getting newly involved in tree planting schemes has withered and died along with the trees they sought to nurture. Sound practical advice based on first hand experience is essential to the success of tree planting schemes and woodland management and it is this advice which this Handbook seeks to provide.

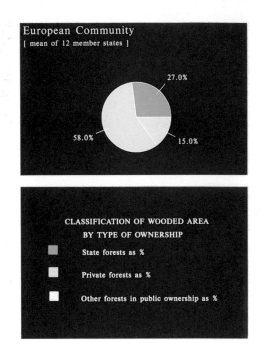

FIGURE 1.1
Forest ownership within the European Community.
Redrawn from Forestry Statistics on the European Community, a chart appearing on the map *The European Community Forests*, with permission of the copyright holder the Commission of the European Communities.

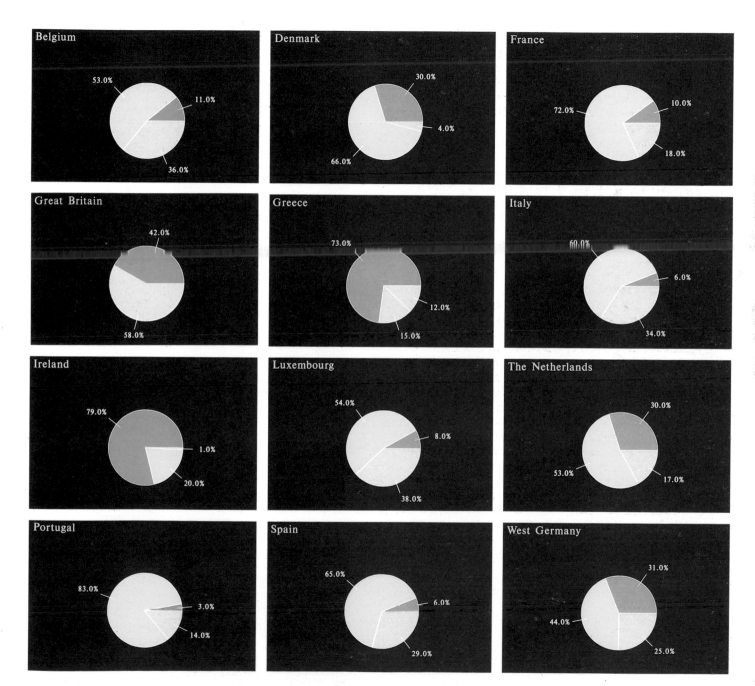

Belgium
53.0%
11.0%
36.0%

Denmark
30.0%
4.0%
66.0%

France
72.0%
10.0%
18.0%

Great Britain
42.0%
58.0%

Greece
73.0%
12.0%
15.0%

Italy
60.0%
6.0%
34.0%

Ireland
79.0%
1.0%
20.0%

Luxembourg
54.0%
8.0%
38.0%

The Netherlands
30.0%
53.0%
17.0%

Portugal
83.0%
3.0%
14.0%

Spain
65.0%
6.0%
29.0%

West Germany
31.0%
44.0%
25.0%

38286

PLATE 4
Deliberate vandalism.

38310

PLATE 5
Unthinking vandalism.

Management plans

Because of the long-term nature of tree growing and the multiple objectives involved, a management plan is essential to any scheme. This need not be a complicated and lengthy document. At its best it is a simple statement of the principal aspects of management which will provide a basis for continuity of practice through changes of stewardship or ownership. In the absence of such a plan the care of trees and especially felling and replacement is often limited to crisis managment.

A simple realistic managment plan will not only ensure continuity of practice but, when prepared at the outset of a scheme, can overcome one of the most difficult problems in urban management, that of planning for tree development. Trees are usually represented on plans for development as though they are architectural features of fixed dimensions. Diagrammatic projections accompanying planning application documents show trees as static at a particular and very limited period in their development and at a particular time of year, e.g. summer, when their size and numbers will be appropriate to the overall design.

The result of this approach is that large species or planting stock are often chosen for planting so that they most nearly match the size envisaged in the plan. Such large trees are expensive, and require intensive care including support in the form of stakes and ties. If the trees survive and grow they will, for perhaps 10 or so years, appear smaller and more widely spaced than was envisaged in the original plan. Then for a relatively short period of time, perhaps another 10 or 15 years, the trees will conform to the design envisaged. After that, as they grow, they will become too large and crowded and questions will arise about how thinning and pruning can be undertaken economically and without damage to the remaining trees. Eventually the trees will become overmature and start to decay due to natural processes. At this last stage they may become a hazard to public safety and property. By then tree replacement will be long overdue and it will be many more years before new trees can once again fulfil the original design concept.

All these problems stem from treating trees solely as landscape objects as though they were non-living architectural elements. The professional forester's approach to tree management, which is explained in detail in this Handbook, recognises the dynamic nature of trees and woodlands and plans managment for not just one short period in the tree's life but for the sequence from small transplant to mature tree and with adequate provision for its succession. This approach to tree management will avoid the need for widespread preservation of overmature and dangerous trees which creates so many difficulties in public areas.

This Handbook relies heavily on the practical experience of foresters and arboriculturists who have first hand knowledge either of growing trees in urban conditions or of managing schemes and contracts, often involving community effort. *A thread running throughout the Handbook is the need to obtain value for money and to avoid waste.* In this connection it is worth noting that all too often the words 'commercial' and 'cost effective' are equated with poor aesthetic quality, while desirable attributes such as good landscape and high conservation value are thought of as costly and unproductive. This attitude can reach absurd proportions in the management of woodlands and trees for non-commercial objectives. It cannot be emphasised too much that those urban woodlands which are a perpetual financial drain are unlikely to survive when the initial enthusiasm and money run out. Bearing in mind the length of a tree's life, it is extremely likely that the type of managment which is entirely dependent on heavy and continuous funding and never offset by income or other benefits generated from the woodland will falter or fail at some stage.

This Handbook proposes a series of management prescriptions aimed at producing robust systems where well chosen trees planted on properly prepared sites will grow healthily with a minimum of aftercare. Chosen carefully for the appropriateness of their location and ultimate size, such trees will provide a continuous but varied setting for housing and industry and most important of all, for people.

2   A short history of urban forestry in Britain

Urban forestry is well established in North America and in parts of Europe, but it remains little appreciated or understood in Britain. In its full sense it involves a wide range of initiatives designed to enrich the urban environment with trees: street trees, garden trees, widely spaced park trees, groups and strips of trees planted for screening, space division, irregular woodlands (such as waterside plantings), for wildlife habitats, with linking corridors; and larger woodland areas managed for various purposes including timber production and quiet recreation. Other benefits include shelter, more varied recreation and educational opportunities, saving in green space maintenance costs, employment, and revenue from timber production. A linked mosaic or network of trees will also bring a feeling of nature into the urban environment.

In most British towns, trees are limited to gardens, streets and parks and in the last they are typically widely spaced in large areas of mown grass. Woodland has seldom been regarded as an essential part of the urban landscape and, with the exception of some new towns, its existence in and around our towns and cities is more often a matter of chance than of design. Woodlands which have been absorbed by expanding towns are generally preserved as landscape features, but few are managed and there is still a widely held misconception that they are self-perpetuating and that management can be limited to emergency work to protect public safety.

The evolution of urban forestry in Britain

Some of the finest tree landscapes in town gardens, squares and crescents were planted many years ago for private enjoyment but these were mainly features of the wealthy middle class areas and poorer residential and industrial areas were largely devoid of trees. It was not until the Victorian era that parks were laid out for public benefit and town dwellers could enjoy landscaped areas which were previously the preserve of the privileged few.

Such parks were usually isolated in large densely built-up areas.

The environmental benefits of trees in cities were perceived at the turn of the century by Ebenezer Howard whose book *Garden cities of tomorrow* inspired the early landscaping of Letchworth and Welwyn Garden City, the forerunners of the New Towns. Both were designed to provide low density building in attractively landscaped surroundings, but regrettably, it was not until the approach of the Second World War that Howard's ideals were more generally adopted. The Government was then becoming increasingly aware of problems in urban areas, and of the need for overall land management planning. This led to the setting up of a Royal Commission in 1937, whose report, the Barlow Report 1940, recommended decentralisation and the easing of congested urban areas. The Barlow Report prescriptions were further developed by Sir Patrick Abercrombie, whose Greater London Plan 1945 proposed three concentric zones around the central built-up area; a low density suburban zone, a green belt, and an outer zone in which new towns would be built.

New Towns

The New Towns Committee chaired by Lord Reith was appointed in 1945. Its second interim report in April 1946 was produced to provide guidance on such matters as land acquisition, finance and the provision of public services prior to the introduction of the New Towns Bill in the same month. The final report in July 1946 dealt with the principles on which a new town should be planned.

Residential areas were planned each with its own shops, parks and other amenities and separated from adjoining 'villages' and industrial zones by broad green areas. There has been some variation in the way development corporations tackled their planning and environmental problems, but most of them have made good use of existing woodland and new plantations for

PLATE 6
Traditional formal landscaping; Lanhydrock, Devon.

screening and landscaping purposes. Twenty-eight new towns have been designated in Britain since 1946 with the third and last generation (which included Milton Keynes), starting in 1967. It is expected that by 1992 the last of the New Town Development Corporations in England and Wales will have been wound up (the position is different for new towns in Scotland).

The overall success of New Town urban forestry can largely be attributed to the administrative stability of the Development Corporations over the last 30–40 years, to their long-term financial arrangements, and to public ownership of land.

Mature towns and cities

Since the mid-1970s the Government's priorities regarding urban improvement have focused on the inner cities. Unlike the New Towns, very little progress has been made in mature towns in urban forestry terms, and indeed the opportunities are often limited by the extent of the built-up areas. But in many urban areas there are large tracts of derelict land, old railways and canals, derelict industrial sites and the spoil of abandoned mines. Not all such areas can be readily planted because some contain excessive concentrations of toxic materials. But in most cases, reclamation techniques are available and urban forestry offers a solution to the rehabilitation of these areas.

The local authorities in Britain's towns and cities have evolved patterns of administration under the influence of ministerial guidelines, local politics, and financial priorities, which allow for consideration of tree and woodland management. Many successful efforts have been and are being made to create new woodlands on waste and derelict land in such places as central Scotland, the north-east of England and the Black Country. However, although many authorities own substantial areas of public open space, they do not have the long-term financial security which the New Towns have enjoyed. It is not uncommon to find local authorities with four or more departments with responsibilities for tree management and no overall tree and woodland management policy, and if funds can be found for tree planting, they may not always be obtainable for necessary aftercare and maintenance.

PLATE 7
Managed woodland in Leeds.

High failure rate of urban trees

There is widespread evidence of poor performance in urban amenity trees and particularly in street trees. Contributory factors include densely compacted unaerated soils, inadequate drainage, grass competition, mowing damage, incorrect stake support, and with street trees lack of soil moisture because of water-sealed surfaces. Poor species selection often necessitates an ongoing and expensive commitment to regular pruning and thinning. Most of these failures can be avoided or significantly reduced by adopting good management practices. The techniques are known, but good techniques alone may not ensure success. Good organisation, and adequate funds to cover maintenance costs, are all-important if urban forestry is to succeed.

Joint forestry survey

A joint survey of urban forestry undertaken by the Forestry Commission and the Countryside Commission in February–June 1988 reported that the majority of the New Town Development Corporations had adopted sound principles of urban forestry, though most of their planting was still immature. A few, such as Cumbernauld, had also planted areas which were scheduled for housing and industrial development in the longer term. These Corporations recognised that woodlands are a growing asset and can yield a useful return even if felled when quite young; that woodlands are cheaper to maintain than other public open spaces, and that the trees retained when the development goes ahead can be very useful for landscaping purposes. It was noted that if no older woodland was available in the designated areas, the appearance of maturity could only be obtained in the short term at considerable. expense. So-called instant trees can be successfully transplanted but they can cost over £1000 each and their use is likely to be justified in a few key positions only. Otherwise the aim must be to establish trees which thrive and grow quickly.

It is apparent from the survey that business investors and house buyers are more likely to be attracted to landscaped areas with well developed trees, and some development corporations have considered that the high costs of the more intensive establishment techniques may be justified if they can quickly produce something approaching the desired appearance of maturity. Such techniques may include 100% pre-planting herbi-cide treatment; pit planting with closely spaced whips, feathered and standard trees; fertilising; protecting and supporting with plastic tree guards or shelters and stakes, with follow-up herbicide weeding, further fertilising, pruning and respacing.

Costs can be as high as £20 000 per hectare to year 8. The survey noted that the basic traditional forestry type of planting, using smaller transplants at 2 m spacing and spot spray herbicide treatment, costs around £2000–£2500 per hectare. The use of treeshelters might increase this to £3000–£3500 per hectare. The survey noted this wide range of costs and made the following observations:

1. the high-cost intensively established plantations quickly reached a thicket stage (usually by about year 5);
2. the wider spaced forestry type plantations were slower to close canopy, but the inter-tree weed growth, which may include bramble and goat willow, provided a more attractive wildlife habitat;
3. if treeshelters or fast-growing tree species were used, smaller transplants quickly caught up and often surpassed the height of the more expensive standard trees.

It is evident from the survey that the benefit-to-cost ratios of the high-cost and low-cost practices are related to the planners' and landscape architects' perceptions of desirable landscaping. A mixed broadleaved tree plantation at 3 × 3 m spacing with a temporary weed in-fill of goat willow may appear untidy to some, but attractive to others. Since the more intensive practices could cost five times as much to establish, one might question whether a little semi-natural 'untidiness' may not justify the adoption of the lower cost methods in some circumstances.

The urban forestry survey team came across a small number of local authorities with excellent examples of urban woodland management. There appears to be a growing awareness that it is unrealistic to treat urban woodland as natural self-perpetuating wilderness. Nevertheless, the overall conclusion was that there had been no significant improvement in urban woodland management since the Forestry Commission's 1979–82 census, and that there is an urgent need for positive tree management and co-ordinated approach in most urban areas.

PLATE 8
Site of the Cymer Afan forest plot near
Port Talbot, West Glamorgan, 1952.

PLATE 9
The Cymer Afan forest plot, 1959.

38785

PLATE 10
The Cymer Afan forest plot, 1969.

PLATE 11
Within the Cymer Afan forest plot, 1988

Urban Forestry and the Community

More than any other aspect of forestry in Britain, urban forestry has to do with the needs and aspirations of people. It must always strive to enlist the enthusiasm and active support of the public. These chapters have been written by two people with first-hand experience and extensive involvement in community projects.

3   Involving the public

It is a paradox in Britain that the publicly owned urban forest has traditionally been managed with very little input from the public themselves. The selection, planting and management of trees were left to local authority staff who provided a service on behalf of the community. If there were few complaints it was generally assumed that the service was admired and appreciated. This rather detached approach to the management of community trees has become increasingly inappropriate.

The provision of urban trees can no longer be regarded as just another public service to be operated with the same degree of detachment as refuse collection. The rapid growth of the voluntary sector over the past decade has resulted in large numbers of locally-based environmental and conservation organisations, amenity societies and other community groups all wanting to be consulted and involved in the management of the trees in their area. At the same time forestry, arboricultural and countryside officers have become painfully aware that not all residents actually appreciate trees or treat them as a community asset. Attitudes of indifference, and even open hostility, towards 'the Council's trees' are now alarmingly common. Vandalism and casual abuse of trees has reached epidemic proportions in some urban areas.

With the development of urban forestry has come a far greater emphasis on the sociological aspects of urban tree management. Indeed, the subject is as much about people as it is about trees. Community forestry programmes, specifically designed to encourage residents to be involved with their publicly-owned trees, are now recognised as an essential element of urban forest policy. Community trees need to be managed with the community and not just for them. This is not simply in the interests of the local authority although improved public relations, greater accountability, reduced levels of vandalism and the availability of voluntary labour undoubtedly contribute to a more efficient and effective service. Most importantly, being involved is of benefit to the community itself. Through community forestry programmes, residents develop a greater awareness, appreciation and sense of responsibility for their trees.

They become part of the decision making process that shapes their environment and can make an active contribution to its improvement.

Education and information

It would however be unrealistic to expect large numbers of urban residents to respond immediately to the opportunity to help plant and care for their publicly owned trees. Of course, there will be members of environmental and conservation groups who will welcome this chance; but for the majority of urban residents, trees are of little significance in their everyday lives. This is especially true in areas dominated by tower blocks and tenements, and in the neglected and depressed inner-cities. Since these residents have virtually no contact with trees they will have little concept of the benefits of urban forestry. The most difficult task for those engaged in promoting community forestry programmes is to generate sufficient interest in trees to motivate residents to become involved. It requires a long-term strategy of education and information.

Notification of proposed work

When major tree work has to be carried out, particularly in residential areas, the local community should be consulted about the work and given a brief explanation of why it is necessary. This is not only good for public relations, it helps to create interest in the trees and reminds residents that trees are a significant feature in the neighbourhood. Unless the work has to be undertaken immediately to ensure the safety of the public, this notification should be given several days in advance so that any questions or objections can be adequately considered. Notification need not be an expensive or time consuming exercise, just a small card or standard letter through the door when the tree has been inspected and the work decided. Alternatively, notification can be given through local community

PLATE 12
Children who learn to play among trees may be less likely to damage them wilfully, but using trees in this way requires careful planning and management.

groups, tree committees or voluntary tree wardens. This avoids the necessity of contacting individual residents and strengthens the role of these groups in the community.

Technical information

Many local authorities produce advisory literature such as posters and leaflets on different aspects of tree planting, care and protection. They are usually directed at property owners with a view to encouraging planting and improving standards of maintenance on private land. However, they can be equally valuable in stimulating interest and providing technical guidelines for community forestry work. Even if they are not used in any practical activity they serve to educate the public about the importance and also the needs of trees.

Exhibitions and displays

Static exhibitions can be mounted in civic centre foyers, libraries, schools and other public buildings. They provide a means of displaying general information, making use of posters and leaflets, or more specific information relating to a particular site or forthcoming event. Some local authorities and voluntary organisations have developed mobile exhibitions, transported in so-called 'tree buses', which can travel around neighbourhoods and estates in support of local community forestry initiatives. An 'Open Day' can be held at the arboricultural depot. Demonstrations of tree planting, climbing and pruning can be staged, which will give the public an insight into the range of equipment and skills required to plant and care for trees. The public have a chance to meet the people who look after their urban forest and ask questions about the work.

Talks and guided walks

Although time consuming to organise and deliver, a talk illustrated with slides can be far more stimulating than an unmanned exhibition. Posters and leaflets can still be displayed at the venue but the presence of a member of the arboricultural staff provides a personal point of contact for the public. Talks should avoid becoming formal lectures, except where appropriate, but attempt instead to create a relaxing and informal atmosphere with plenty of time for discussion and social contact. Guided walks can be conducted through parks, gardens and even streets where there are trees of special interest. The trees should not be presented as just a succession of individual ornamental specimens; their overall management and environmental value should also be emphasised.

Consultation

Consulting the local community about their trees, like educating and informing them, is an important step towards encouraging their full participation. These consultations demonstrate to residents that they have a responsibility for their trees and an effective voice in influencing management. Where residents have been consulted they are also more likely to accept and appreciate the work that follows. Unfortunately their views are often overlooked when designing new planting schemes or formulating management decisions. Obviously few residents have much arboricultural expertise but this does not mean they are incapable of expressing an opinion when presented with a choice of feasible alternatives. It may not be possible, or desirable, to consult residents on an individual basis, except perhaps where the proposed work would have a dramatic effect on their immediate surroundings. However, residents should be consulted regularly on a group basis about major decisions which affect the treescape of their area. A number of methods can be used.

Public meetings

All too often public meetings are called simply to calm angry residents following a controversial decision where they were not consulted. If convened by the local authority in the first instance they can usually defuse a potentially difficult situation before it develops. Apart from their 'trouble-shooting' role, public meetings also allow residents to engage in open and frank discussion with officers and councillors on a range of issues affecting the urban forest. Unfortunately, there is the danger of public meetings turning into 'informing' sessions only, providing superficial information, discouraging questions or even giving irrelevant answers. A poor attendance may mean that a lack of publicity has left many residents unaware that the meeting is taking place. But it can also be a reflection of the public's mistrust in the purpose of the meeting and a belief that nothing will actually change as a result. However, when meetings are

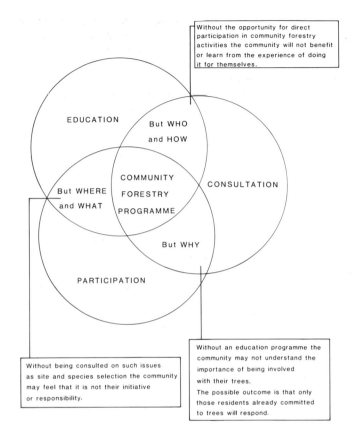

FIGURE 3.1

A community forestry programme should include a balance of education, consultation and participation strategies. If any of the three elements is not represented, the impact of the programme is likely to be limited.

organised in a genuine effort to consult the public they can be very constructive. A small attendance need not indicate a lack of interest as many of the people present may be acting as spokespersons for local voluntary organisations and community groups. In this way the views of a large number of people can be represented without the need for them to attend the meeting itself. This can even speed up the process of consultation.

Community group discussions

These are usually far more successful than public meetings in allowing individuals and groups to make personal contact with officers. Formal public meetings can inhibit people from expressing their views. But these more informal gatherings with fewer people present stimulate better communication. This form of consultation can take place in the home of a local resident or at the particular site that is the subject of the discussion. They are especially appropriate where a difficult decision may have to be taken to remove or drastically prune trees. The presence of the trees will assist the officer to explain the problem and reach an understanding with the residents. This type of meeting is also useful in community tree planting schemes where the initial response may have been through a reply slip on a leaflet. A follow-up telephone conversation can culminate in an on-site meeting between an officer and representatives of the local group expressing an interest in the scheme. The meeting assesses the needs of the community and leads to advice and discussions about possible plans for the site.

Tree committees

An increasing number of local authorities are establishing borough-wide tree committees made up of representatives from interested voluntary organisations and the larger community groups together with officers and a few councillors. In some cases the local authority side may only be present in an advisory capacity or as observers. The committees meet regularly and serve as a forum for consultation and discussion about topical issues affecting the urban forest. They generally have no real power to make decisions and are limited to recommendations which the local authority may, or may not, choose to follow. Because of this they run the risk of becoming 'talking-shops', with the community representatives slowly losing interest,

particularly if their recommendations are frequently ignored. However, the potential exists to develop these tree committees into a genuine partnership between the community and the local authority where the public can participate in the development of urban forestry policy.

Participation in a practical way

Direct public participation in the work of the forestry and arboricultural services is one of the most beneficial forms of community involvement, especially for those residents without their own trees and gardens. In selecting and planting trees they gain the satisfaction of improving their environment and making a personal imprint on the landscape. By caring for their own trees they develop positive attitudes towards other trees. Their increased awareness and appreciation encourages a sense of responsibility for trees that motivates a concern for their care and protection. Participation in community forestry activities can also have a beneficial effect on the social life of the community. It improves social contact between residents by bringing them together in a creative atmosphere.

Participation need not be restricted to the planting of trees. Although there are obvious limitations imposed by safety and the degree of training required, the scope is still considerable. However, the actual level of community involvement in these activities can vary enormously as much depends on how they are organised and operated.

Sponsor-a-tree schemes and tree appeals

Many local authorities run sponsorship schemes or tree appeals which allow individual residents, community groups and local businesses to make donations for tree planting. However, these schemes rarely involve the public in the actual planting of the trees and are simply a request for funds to facilitate tree planting by local authority staff. A few schemes do allow some choice in the selection of species and planting site. Although these schemes may have a valid purpose in getting trees planted, in their present form the level of community involvement is usually minimal. The opportunity exists to dramatically increase their impact by not only allowing direct participation in the planting but actually encouraging it.

PLATE 13
School children planting trees as part of a conservation project;
Farnborough, Hampshire.

Community tree planting

Involving residents in the selection and planting of trees is perhaps the most common form of public participation. It is a creative and educational activity in which almost everyone can take part, often in large numbers. But the success of community tree planting events depends on careful planning and organisation. The details of the site and the size, number and species of trees to be planted should be agreed between officers and representatives of the community group well before the planting date. The event must then be given plenty of advance publicity to ensure the attendance of sufficient numbers of residents. A supply of tools and planting materials has to be organised together with the arrangements for adequate supervision of the work by experienced personnel. Locally based conservation organisations can often help with these aspects of the event thus easing the burden of the work on the local authority.

Community tree planting events should do more than simply provide an opportunity for people to plant trees. With a little imagination and enterprise they can be transformed into colourful social occasions. Community artists and musicians can be invited to entertain the crowd and amuse the children. Conservation and environmental organisations can be asked to erect stalls and small displays. The forestry and arboricultural section itself can give demonstrations of tree care equipment and techniques. These and other ideas can be used to create an atmosphere that is entertaining and educational. Inviting local dignitaries or a well known personality to attend the event can substantially increase attendance. However, the fact that people turn up to an event does not constitute their full participation; everyone should be encouraged to take an active part in the tree planting.

Aftercare

Participation need not end once residents have planted their own trees. The community group that carried out the planting should be encouraged to undertake the post-planting work necessary to ensure that the trees survive and become established. Adjusting tree ties and removing stakes (where these are used), even weeding and formative pruning can all be done by volunteers provided they have been given some instructions. However, the work needs to be monitored carefully to be certain that the trees receive attention and are not just forgotten. Someone in the community group should be nominated to organise sufficient volunteers or inform the local authority if additional help is needed.

Residents may also be interested in working on trees they did not plant themselves. Every year thousands of young trees planted by local authority staff either die or are severely damaged because it has not been possible to ensure adequate maintenance. A little help from the community could dramatically improve this situation.

Tree wardens

Establishing a system of voluntary tree wardens is an extremely useful way of allowing a limited number of residents to become quite heavily involved. Each warden covers a small part of the local authority area such as a neighbourhood, housing estate or electoral ward. Their main role is to act as a link between the local authority and the public and generally take a lead in developing community forestry activities in their area. Being the local tree warden can be quite demanding, and not just in terms of time and commitment to the work. It requires someone who not only has a reasonable knowledge of trees but also the necessary social skills to communicate with residents and community groups. But it can be enormously rewarding work and it should be possible to find enough suitable volunteers from among the membership of local conservation and environmental groups and amenity societies. Although the system may take a little time to establish it should more than repay that effort.

Tree nurseries

A number of community tree nurseries have recently been set up, often on local authority land but run by local conservation groups. They involve residents in a wide range of activities from collecting seed through to the distribution of the trees for community planting schemes. They often have close links with the schools in their area and parties of children regularly visit the nursery to help with the work and receive instruction in nursery practices as part of their studies.

PLATE 14
The Forest of London Project – poster for a tree planting day.

Initiating and implementing programmes

In this chapter a range of community forestry initiatives has been described. The list is by no means exhaustive but gives an outline of the major schemes and strategies currently in use. Each initiative should not be viewed in isolation but as part of an overall community forestry programme containing a wide variety of measures. To attempt to encourage the more sophisticated forms of participation without also promoting a wide ranging education and information programme can lead to rather limited results. Those organisations and individuals who are already interested in trees will tend to dominate the programme while the vast majority of residents continue to remain unmoved. To achieve widespread community involvement also requires a long-term effort, particularly among residents who have little awareness or experience of trees. It may be tempting to concentrate resources in the leafy and affluent residential districts where fairly quick results can be obtained. But it is the residents living in the neglected and depressed neighbourhoods where there are few trees or private gardens who will, in the long term, benefit most from involvement.

Initiating and implementing a community forestry programme will require publicity and additional financial resources and manpower. Fortunately, most do not have to start from scratch but can build on the various activities already taking place. They can also make the most of existing resources and facilities.

Publicity and the media

Community forestry programmes must be widely publicised. Most local authorities have a publicity department which can design posters and leaflets, prepare and distribute press releases, and liaise with the local media. The participation of the media can dramatically increase the impact of a programme by giving advance publicity to events and activities, reporting on them when they happen and highlighting the positive results achieved. Local newspapers should be asked to carry items of interest about trees, regularly featuring items such as a report on a particularly rare or historic tree, or a feature on the work of the arboricultural section. It provides valuable support for other activities by keeping trees in the public eye. Many of the larger community groups will have their own contacts with the local media and will generate their own publicity for events and activities where they are involved.

Mark Johnson

PLATE 15
The participation of well-known personalities and the media can
dramatically increase the impact of a community forest initiative.
Here, Richard Branson is being interviewed by Thames Television after
climbing to the top of the tallest tree in central London to publicise the
'Forest of London' project.

Financial resources

Limited finances within many urban local authorities may discourage the development of greater community involvement. Services are under pressure and there are many demands on the scarce resources. The arboricultural service may be given a low priority and even routine tree maintenance may be pared down to meet a reduced spending target. Where arboricultural sections receive insufficient funding to pursue an effective community involvement policy, contact with the public becomes increasingly a result of complaints about long delays in dealing with less urgent work.

In the long term, community forestry can make a valuable contribution to the resources available to the arboricultural section but it does require an initial investment and one which may take some time to bear fruit. There has to be the political will on the part of councillors to make that investment and protect it. A stop-start approach to community involvement can be almost as damaging as no policy at all. In recent years central government has encouraged community-based environmental projects, particularly in inner-city areas. Local government initiatives in community forestry may be subject to grant support. The major voluntary organisations who are keen to participate can often obtain grants on their own behalf and sponsorship from local businesses is an important source of funding which is increasingly being explored.

Manpower

The most effective way of initiating a community forestry programme would be to create a post of Community Tree Officer and appoint someone who has experience in this field. Unfortunately, for many local authorities this may not be possible unless funding for the post can come from an outside source. The initial burden of starting the programme may have to be carried by existing staff. However, it would be a mistake to believe that once interest has been aroused the major part of the work involved in promoting and running the programme would continue to fall on the local authority. The underlying aim of community forestry is to encourage residents to do as much as possible for themselves.

Local authority staff should act as a catalyst for community action by building contacts with organisations and individuals who are already sympathetic and encouraging them to take a lead in the development of the programme. The major voluntary organisations that are concerned with conservation and the environment can be particularly helpful. Many of their full-time staff are funded by government sponsored employment schemes and participation in community forestry initiatives offers them an excellent opportunity to increase their numbers. They can offer training in a wide range of skills to individual residents and community groups who want to take part in the programme.

4   Community events and projects

Successful community involvement relies upon professional staff responding to public interest and encouraging action from the community.

Each urban forestry project is unique. However, it is possible to distinguish two main forms of community involvement each of which is suited to fulfilling a specific set of requirements. The following table analyses the advantages and disadvantages of short and longer term projects.

Table 4.1

Short-term projects	Long-term projects
Resources are required for a relatively short time only.	Long-term resource commitment is required.
An interesting event can focus the attention of local people and provide PR opportunities.	A succession of interesting and relevant events is required with possibilities for a build-up of PR.
When the event is over community involvement usually comes to an end.	Can lead to the creation of community woodland groups.
Community interest in trees may be fitful and discontinuous.	People are encouraged to take a continuing interest in the site and to care for it.
Organisational skills are required.	Community development skills are required in addition to organisational skills.

Short-term community participation projects

Single short-term events are of great use to an organisation which cannot put permanent resources (staff materials or money) into a project on a continuing basis. Such events include community tree planting days, which are one of the most frequent forms of community involvement. Generally, the aims of such projects are to provide an enjoyable event for local people which will create a good image for trees locally, generating some press coverage and possibly leading to less vandalism on the site.

People can achieve a lot in a day if the organisation and appropriate tools are set-up in advance. Work with axes, bill hooks or other edged tools should be avoided, and a chainsaw should be operated only under strict safety rules and by a trained and skilled operator. Large projects which would swamp the resources available to a relatively inexperienced group of individuals, should be divided into achievable sub-projects.

Planning notes

BEFORE THE DAY

1. Decide who will be in charge of the event. Consider bringing in help from one of the voluntary organisations.
2. Remember that trees, tools, skips, etc., need to be ordered and arranged up to 2 months in advance, especially if the event is timed to take place at a popular time of year, such as in National Tree Week.
3. Inform local people 7–14 days before the event using leaflets, posters and local papers (include a map to show where the site is, or use road names to pinpoint the location).
4. Arrange first aid cover and insurance.
5. Choose weekends; times between 10.00 am and 4.30 pm.
6. Avoid Bank Holidays, and holiday periods in general. People tend to have made other arrangements on these days.

7. People will tend to come and go in waves throughout the day. Many will be late arriving or will leave early. Prepare the event accordingly. It will be better to arrange for a guest celebrity to attend at a time of peak activity rather than to give an opening speech.

ON THE DAY

1. Make sure that the overall organiser is clearly identified, and that there are enough professionals present to communicate with participants informally.

2. Set realistic targets. Keep people informed about their performance against the targets and celebrate when you have reached them.

Long-term community participation projects

Long-term projects encourage local people to care for the site, to take an interest in it, and to use it in a wide range of appropriate ways, both when the project is launched and in the future. These projects can ensure that someone is always keeping an eye on the site and can lead to the creation of local volunteer work forces if the members of the community feel it is worth their while.

Developing autonomy

The most successful community involvement projects fulfil the needs of the community. They quickly cease to be a plan implemented by one or two keen professionals and they take on a life of their own. These are the projects which are organised and run by local people.

In order to focus attention on a long-term project, it is necessary to employ topics of local concern and interest, examples of such topics include:

1. change of ownership and how the new owners will hope to manage the site;

2. tree felling or surgery work that is planned for the near future;

3. a rubbish clearance campaign;

4. the need for a children's play area;

5. planning applications affecting local trees, and any major work in nearby woodland.

People should be encouraged to think about the future. Following a single event a follow-up meeting can be suggested with the theme "what shall we do next?". It is important to think of the site as a community resource and so the needs for social events as well as work events should be remembered.

In the early stages an experienced and skilled leader is required who can encourage local people to develop their skills and decision making abilities. As time goes on (perhaps after two or three successful events) people should be encouraged to form a group or association which can run its own business and liaise with professionals as appropriate. The group when formed should be encouraged to set clear aims. The move to autonomy should be achieved by the gradual delegation of tasks rather than a sudden withdrawal of professional help.

Planting on bare land

A long-term project for woodland on a bare land site is perhaps the most difficult community involvement to initiate and to develop to the stage where it is self-organising. Unless well designed, the scheme will not fire the enthusiasm of the community.

Any major tree planting initiative runs the risk of completely changing an important community resource. Even apparently unused areas can be important to the local community: for walking the dog; as a short cut to the shops; as a playground; or even just as a clear patch of space to look across from the kitchen window. Trees could be seen as a threat to these amenities and in this case people are going to be reluctant to accept a new resource which will take at least 20 years to look at all impressive.

Most vandalism of trees occurs when the trees are in the wrong place. So a long-term community involvement project in tree planting on a bare site needs to start at the planning stage. Through the public meetings and consultation described in Chapter 3 it is possible to find out what people want to use the site for, and to find ways by which tree planting can play a part in the scheme. This may require parts of the site to be left unplanted. Open spaces and play areas are important and so are view lines through the site once the trees have grown. Three dimensional models of the site can be very useful for deciding where the trees should be planted.

If people feel that the site has become their own community resource it will be quite easy to encourage them to continue to play a role in looking after the site in future. However, it may not always be possible to achieve this degree of participation, and the consultation process may lead to no more than a feeling of general appreciation for the work being carried out. In this case it is unlikely that the community will wish to adopt the site in the long term. However, the scheme will still have a much better chance of success than it would if local people had not been involved in the planning stage.

Preparation and Planting

Unsuitable choice of species, incorrect site preparation, inappropriate planting stock and poor planting practice are the main reasons for failure in urban forestry. Chapters 5 to 7 are intended to provide essential basic advice for planning prior to planting. Chapter 8 deals with operations on site.

5 The new site

Many urban sites will require substantial site preparation, including the importation of soil materials or the modification of existing ones. Soil compaction and drainage usually require attention but soil chemical properties are likely to be adequate except on contaminated sites or those without topsoil.

Sites for tree planting

The sites available for urban forestry are so diverse as to test the skill of the most experienced forester. They range from grass verges between suburban roads and pavements, and urban renewal schemes to old landfill sites, regraded colliery spoil tips and restored gravel pits. In these examples soil materials and site conditions are likely to be very different from one site to another. Table 5.1 lists potential planting sites as related to the scale of planting.

Tree planting in urban areas is notoriously prone to failure; in many cases this is due to inhospitable site conditions. However, although failure can be caused by problems such as toxic soil materials, in most instances it is a lack of understanding of a tree's needs that is at the centre of the problem. Too often simple procedures for site improvement before tree planting are missed out, and bad site preparation will increase the chance of failure; poor choice of soil materials imported on to the site, or compaction of soil by heavy machinery, are examples of bad practice.

Requirements of the tree

Although trees will vary in their site requirements, all have basic needs. These can be grouped under the following headings:
    water supply;
    oxygen supply;
    nutrient supply;
    anchorage.

Trees differ little from other plants in respect of the first three of these requirements. But the tree's need for long term anchorage is often forgotten. Deep and prolific rooting is a necessity for tree stability as the tree grows and puts up greater resistance to the wind. In natural soils, mature trees of most species will root to at least 1 m in depth and some deep rooting ones may root 3 m. Roots will extend well beyond the limit of the crown in erect species like birch, and roughly to the edge of the crown in species like oak and beech. In fact, tree growth and health are very dependent upon the tree's ability to develop an extensive root system with which to extract water and nutrients from the soil.

Water supply

Trees need water, not least because they are mostly made of it. Water is also crucial in biochemical reactions and for the transport of dissolved materials within the tree, and from the soil into the tree. British trees are dependent on supplies of water held in the soil for almost all their needs; very little is absorbed by the leaves or woody parts, almost all entering the tree through the root system.

Soils vary considerably in the amount of water they can contain. As a general rule, the more coarse particles the soil contains, as in sands and gravels, the less water is held in the pores between them. So clay soils, mostly composed of particles less than 2 μm (thousandths of a millimetre), hold considerable amounts of water. However, water supply to the tree is controlled more by the suction exerted by the soil on the water, and the corresponding 'pull' that the tree must exercise to extract the water from the soil. Clay soils, although potentially containing the most moisture, hold it so strongly that only a proportion is released for uptake. In contrast, loamy soils allow much of their water to be taken up. Water content and supply will also be affected by the organic matter content and soil structure or lack of these.

Table 5.1 Where to plant trees: examples of locations and opportunities for tree planting in and around towns and cities, related to scale of planting

	Large scale Individual schemes greater than 0.25 ha or 500 trees	Medium scale Individual schemes around 0.25 ha or 500 trees	Small scale Individual schemes of fewer than 500 trees and down to single trees
Locations	Urban fringe Farm woodlands Reclaimed spoil heaps Reclaimed mineral workings Abandoned quarries Old allotments Major road schemes Existing urban woodlands	Parks Other recreation/play areas Urban road and street schemes Reclaimed factory sites Housing and commercial/ industrial developments Railway land Inner city development projects Golf courses	City centre developments Office blocks Shopping precincts Formal gardens Private gardens Out-of-town supermarkets Recreation grounds Housing estates Car parks Roundabouts

Opportunities	Timber production/firewood
	Major recreation developments
	Wildlife conservation
		Landscape improvement
		Screening
		Shelter
		Development of urban green
		  space
			Decorative and ornamental
			  plantings
			Softening of harsh architectural
			  features
			Development of small-scale
			  green space in heavily
			  developed zones

Species choice	For examples of suitable species see Table 6.2 left-hand column	For examples of suitable species see Table 6.2 middle column	For examples of suitable species see Table 6.2 right-hand column

42

PLATES 16–18
Industrial reclamation sites pose severe problems for urban forestry.

Oxygen supply

All plants need oxygen to respire, and trees are no exception. Respiration takes place throughout the living parts of a tree, including the roots. In natural well drained soils, oxygen can account for 15–20% of the total soil gases, and respiration takes place unhindered. However, in many urban soils subject to waterlogging or compaction, little pore space remains to contain oxygen. These soils are very susceptible to anaerobism, and tree roots may die when this occurs. In perpetually waterlogged soils, the root system and, in due course, the whole tree will die. Tree species vary to some extent in their tolerance of waterlogging; alders are well known examples of trees able to grow in seasonally wet soils. However, tolerant trees are usually shallow rooted, and therefore prone to summer drought, and windthrow. In general, all trees grow better in aerated soils.

Nutrient supply

Soils are a mixture of mineral and organic materials. Both contribute essential nutrients that a tree takes up via its root system. All tree species require the same basic set of nutrients, although these requirements will vary both in total and relative proportions between species. The nutrients required are nitrogen (as nitrate and ammonium), phosphorus (as phosphate), potassium, calcium, sulphur (as sulphate), magnesium, iron, manganese, copper, boron, chlorine (as chloride), zinc and molybdenum. Natural soils differ somewhat in their ability to supply these nutrients. The greatest differences are between soils containing free calcium carbonate (alkaline soils) and those which do not (acidic soils). The acidity or alkalinity of a soil is most conveniently described using the soil pH scale: soils with a pH less than 7 tend towards acidity, whilst those with a pH greater than 7 are alkaline.

37623

37624

PLATE 19
Soil compaction assessment using a penetrometer.

PLATE 20
Soil gas analysis using an oxylarm meter and probe.

Properties of urban soils

Man-made or altered soils are often deficient in some essential elements. The permanent removal of topsoil does the most damage to a soil's ability to grow trees, because most of the nitrogen and phosphorus exist in this upper layer. Other deficiencies are comparatively rare, even in the most disturbed soils and spoils.

Urban soils may contain a wide range of materials not normally found in natural soils. These may be landfill materials like domestic wastes, or sewage sludge or a wide range of industrial products and wastes. The most offensive materials contain phytotoxic elements such as cadmium, lead, nickel and mercury; some sites may be contaminated by coal tar, cyanide or phenolic compounds. Some so-called inert materials like builders' rubble, concrete and asphalt can be tolerated in the soil, but many pollutants will kill trees if present in anything more than very small amounts. There are few guidelines on critical levels of such materials partly because availability is affected by other soil factors like pH and organic matter content and partly because tree species differ in their uptake and tolerance of such materials. Table 5.2 shows EEC threshold values for heavy metals which should be used as guidelines.

Natural soils develop over thousands of years. During this time the action of plant roots and soil animals, together with wetting and drying and freezing and thawing cycles, have led to

Table 5.2 Limit value for concentrations of heavy metals in soil

Metal	Limit value (mg/kg dry matter)
Cadmium	1–3
Copper	50–140
Nickel	30–75
Lead	50–300
Zinc	150–300
Mercury	1–1.5
Chromium	100–200

soils with well developed soil structure. Soils comprise aggregates of mineral and organic matter which vary widely in size, and are separated from one another over much of their surface by pores, fissures and cracks. Urban soils are often subject to processes which reverse the development of soil structure. Soil materials can be compressed by heavy machinery or even pedestrian traffic. Most compaction is induced if soils are moved about, especially when wet. Soil movement is commonplace on sites used for mineral extraction and soils may be transported several times before final replacement. Large and heavy plant such as boxscrapers and dump trucks are often used in these operations; these can weigh over 100 tonnes fully laden, and they exert very large ground pressures.

Compaction may also be induced by deliberate action, for example in embankments, to reduce porosity and increase soil strength and stability. Colliery spoil tips, too, may be compacted to reduce the risk of spontaneous combustion within the tip. Unless remedial action is taken before planting, trees will only root in the uppermost soil layers on these sites, and tree growth and health will be put at risk. There is no evidence that trees can penetrate compacted soils better than other plant types.

Improving the site for tree planting

Soil selection

Some urban forestry sites have little soil material *in situ*; either soils are buried by concrete, asphalt, brick or similar materials,

by waste from mineral extraction, or they have been exported from the site. Alternatively, contamination may make existing soils unusable. In these circumstances, it is likely that other soil or 'soil-forming' materials will need to be imported on to the site. It is necessary to distinguish between different types of soil material commonly used, particularly 'topsoil', 'subsoil' and 'overburden'.

Topsoil is the darker organic-rich material, commonly up to 20 cm thick which occurs at the soil surface. Subsoil is the soil material below the topsoil, generally to about 100 cm depth. Both materials are usually well structured, though the former is by far the most fertile. The term overburden is commonly used for materials overlying workable minerals or aggregates; overburden is usually massively structured and far less fertile than either topsoil or subsoil. It should only be used as a material for tree planting if soils are not available or unusable; its use is likely to restrict the range of species that can be grown.

British Standards for topsoil are presently under revision and will give useful guidelines on quality. Table 5.3 outlines desirable soil properties in imported material. Clays should be avoided whenever possible as they are likely to lead to problems of waterlogging. It is important, too, to ensure that imported materials are not themselves contaminated and toxic to trees.

Table 5.3 Desirable soil properties in imported soil materials

1. **Texture**: sands silts and loams with less than 40% clay (<2 µm)

2. **Soil reaction**: pH 4.0–8.0

3. **Stone content**: less than 30% by dry weight; stones less than 50 mm in size

4. **Other inclusions**: free of weed seeds, roots of perennial weeds, sticks and foreign matter

5. **Electrical conductivity**: below 2 mS/cm (1:1 spoil:water suspension)

6. **Heavy metal content**: below EEC limit values (Table 5.2)

PLATE 21
Successful tree planting on a reclaimed derelict colliery and pit heap,
Co. Durham.

Amelioration of site conditions

Physical properties

If compaction is present it must be overcome. Ways to do this will depend on the site and its size. In the suburban street it may be difficult to do more than excavate a large planting pit to allow soil materials to be replaced in a loose state. On embankments, too, engineering constraints prevent complete ground preparation.

On larger sites, complete ground preparation should be seen as the ideal to work towards. This is obtained by ripping or subsoiling the ground in summer months when the soil is driest. Because deep rooting is desirable for long-term health, ripping should be performed as deep as possible. The efficacy will depend on soil and site conditions: in dry soils ripping to 75 cm may be possible. However, if the soil is at all wet, ripping may fail to relieve compaction. Ripping to depths of less than 50 cm is unsatisfactory for tree planting schemes, and in wet summers ripping and tree planting should be postponed. Winged tines, now commonly available, should be used to extend the lateral effect of ripping. Agricultural machinery is rarely strong enough for these operations, and a tracked dozer should be used, employing two or three tines, two placed behind the dozer tracks to counteract any compaction the dozer might induce. Once ripping has taken place, traversing the ground should be avoided – ground for tree planting need not be as even and uniform as that required for other land uses.

New research is beginning to show that there are substantial benefits where compaction, and hence the need for ripping, can be avoided altogether. On sites where soil materials will be moved and replaced, dump trucks can be used to lay down the soil, and long-arm excavators standing at the side of the soil dumps can be used to spread them without traversing the newly laid ground. This 'loose tipping' approach makes ripping unnecessary.

Many urban sites where tree planting might be contemplated are flat or only gently sloping, for example grass verges between road and pavement, or derelict land adjoining railways or canals. Trees planted on these sites run the risk of waterlogging, especially if soil materials are clayey, groundwater-tables are high or the soil is at all compacted. Sites in depressions are particularly prone to waterlogging. If possible, trees should be planted on banks raised above the water-table. These should have slopes not less than 5–6 degrees in order to promote lateral drainage.

On sites where earthmoving is involved, e.g. regraded colliery spoil tips, or sand and gravel pits, there is more opportunity to provide suitably sloping land for tree planting. Maximum slopes will depend on the engineering properties of the material, and whether the site is to be covered in low vegetation as well as trees. In general, slopes greater than 1 in 3 (19 degrees) run the risk of erosion, and slopes less than 1 in 10 (5 degrees) are prone to waterlogging in winter. Long slopes (more than 20 m or so) should also be avoided to reduce the risk of erosion; slopes longer than this can be interrupted by cut-off drains running close to the contour.

Where the general ground slope is less than 1 in 10, experience has shown that for relatively impermeable materials mounds or ridges constructed purposely will be beneficial. Ridges 30 m wide by 1–1.5 m high have been used successfully. If the mounds can be formed with few or no machine passes by a loose tipping method, compaction will be minimised.

Chemical properties

Some soil chemical properties, such as deficiencies in nitrogen and phosphate, are amenable to correction using artificial fertilisers or sewage sludge. However, these types of ameliorant are not long-lasting and repeated applications are likely to be necessary. In many cases, it is probably a better policy to choose tree species which will tolerate the site in question rather than attempt to change the site to accommodate a particular species or set of species. On sites lacking topsoil, it is more sensible to select nitrogen-fixing tree species such as the alders than to begin a programme of frequent fertiliser applications. Other sites without adequate thickness of soil cover, for example colliery spoil, may require more drastic treatment. Extreme acidity (pH often less than 3) in these materials must be countered by liming, sometimes at rates of 40 tonnes per hectare, before any tree planting can be contemplated. Heavy metal toxicity is more difficult to treat, though liming will reduce the solubility of some elements such as zinc, cadmium, copper, nickel and chromium. Boron toxicity, a possible problem in soils containing pulverised fuel ash (PFA), can also be reduced by liming, though boron is quite easily lost by leaching after a few years.

6 Choice of species

Preparations

The decision on which species to plant should not be made hastily nor should the species simply be used out of habit. Many books are available which describe species and cultivars suitable for growing in Britain and a selection of these is listed on pp. 49–62. This chapter draws attention to the considerations which must be made and provides, in tabular form, check-lists of recommendations related to soil, site, shelter and certain key characteristics of the species listed.

Reference to texts, visiting parks, gardens and arboreta and becoming generally familiar with species is all part of the preparation helpful to reaching decisions over species choice. Planting for timber production in woodlands is sensibly limited to a few conifers and broadleaves and descriptions of these can be found in all standard forestry books; no further comment on them is added here.

One other preliminary point should be made. On some sites there may be existing trees which might serve the purpose just as well as newly planted ones. For example, where natural regeneration of tree and shrub species is present, it will often be both more economical and more rewarding to make the best of this woody growth than to clear it and then carry out new planting.

Importance of correct choice

Well over 1000 species and cultivars are suitable in urban forestry plantings. A selection of these is given in Table 6.1.

The first question to ask is the purpose of the planting, thereafter one can consider which of the trees meeting this requirement are suitable for the site in question. It is important to get these two steps right so that the tree will do the job for which it is planted and will grow with reasonable vigour and in good health. This appears to state the obvious – but all too frequently urban tree plantings look ragged with sickly trees,

and are a poor advertisement often inviting vandalism. Unlike grass cover, and herbaceous and shrubby vegetation (which can often recover from damage in a few weeks, following a new flush of foliage), a sickly, dying tree can hang on for many years as a perpetual reminder of bad practice and wasteful expenditure.

Tree planting schemes in urban areas will usually form part of an overall plan in the development or re-development of the location concerned. At the stage of drawing-up that plan it should be possible to identify the objectives of the tree planting, and then desirable tree characteristics necessary to achieve those objectives should start to become clear. Consideration of the approximate size, rate of growth, shape, colour, shade-bearing characteristics and other key features, will quickly narrow down the range of species suitable for the purpose so that a short list of potentially useful trees can be drawn-up.

Table 6.1 Visual aid to tree selection

	Key to symbols used in table
No mark	Not recommended. Unsuitable for conditions; features not significant.
●	Not recommended. Tolerates conditions but not well suited; features slightly developed.
●	Recommended. Grows adequately; suitable for conditions and site; notable features.
●	Strongly recommended. Thrives; amongst best for site; outstanding features.
A	Notable for autumn colours
D	Deciduous (conifers)
E	Evergreen (broadleaves)

BROADLEAVES

SPECIES/CULTIVAR	SOIL					SITE					SHELTER			FEATURES			
	Wet soils	Clay soils	Chalk soils	Dry sandy soils	Industrial spoils	Seaside	Exposed sites	Smoke and fumes	Small spaces	Roads and streets	Hedges	Screens	Shelter belts	Flowers	Fruit	Bark	Leaves
Acacia dealbata		●	●	●		●	●							●		●	● E
Acer campestre	●	●	●	●	●	●	●	●			●		●				● A
A. davidii	●	●	●	●			●	●								●	● A
A. hersii	●	●	●	●		●	●	●							●	●	● A
A. lobelii		●	●			●	●	●	●	●							
A. macrophyllum	●		●	●		●	●	●									●
A. negundo 'Variegatum'	●	●	●	●		●	●	●	●	●							●
'Auratum'	●	●	●	●		●		●		●							●
A. nikoense		●	●	●					●					●	●		● A
A. platanoides	●	●	●	●	●	●	●	●		●		●	●	●			● A
'Schwedleri'	●	●	●	●			●	●		●				●			● A
'Drummondii'	●	●	●	●		●	●	●		●							●
A. pseudoplatanus	●	●	●	●	●	●	●	●		●		●	●				
'Worleei'	●	●	●	●	●	●	●	●		●							●
A. rubrum	●	●		●			●			●			●	●			● A
A. saccharinum	●	●	●	●	●		●			●	●	●					● A
'Laciniatum'	●	●	●	●			●			●							●
A. saccharum	●	●	●	●						●							● A
A. velutinum																	
var. *vanvolxemii*		●	●	●		●	●	●									●
Aesculus × carnea	●	●	●	●		●	●	●		●				●			
'Briotii'	●	●	●	●		●	●	●		●				●			
A. flava	●	●	●	●		●	●	●						●			● A
A. hippocastanum	●	●	●	●	●	●	●	●		●				●	●		

● STRONGLY RECOMMENDED   ● RECOMMENDED   ● NOT RECOMMENDED

SPECIES/CULTIVAR	SOIL					SITE					SHELTER			FEATURES			
	Wet soils	Clay soils	Chalk soils	Dry sandy soils	Industrial spoils	Seaside	Exposed sites	Smoke and fumes	Small spaces	Roads and streets	Hedges	Screens	Shelter belts	Flowers	Fruit	Bark	Leaves
A. indica	●	●	●	●				●	●					●	●		●
'Sydney Pearce'	●	●	●	●				●	●					●	●		●
A. turbinata	●	●	●	●		●	●	●						●	●		● A
Ailanthus altissima		●	●	●	●	●	●	●		●			●	●	●		●
Alnus cordata	●	●	●	●	●	●	●	●		●	●	●		●	●		
A. glutinosa	●	●	●	●	●	●	●	●	●		●	●		●			
A. incana	●	●	●	●	●		●	●	●	●	●	●		●			
'Aurea'	●	●	●	●			●	●									●
'Pendula'	●	●	●	●	●		●	●	●								
'Ramulis-Coccineis'	●	●	●	●	●		●									●	
A. rubra	●	●	●		●	●		●	●				●				
A. subcordata	●	●	●								●	●					
Betula jacquemontii	●	●	●	●		●	●	●	●					●			
B. lutea	●	●		●			●									●	A
B. maximowicziana	●	●		●			●									●	●
B. nigra	●	●		●						●						●	
B. papyrifera		●		●			●	●	●							●	
B. pendula	●	●	●	●	●	●	●	●	●	●			●			●	A
'Dalecarlica'	●	●	●	●	●	●	●	●	●	●						●	A
'Youngii'	●	●	●	●		●	●	●	●	●						●	
B. pubescens	●	●	●	●	●		●	●	●	●			●				
B. utilis	●	●		●		●	●	●								●	● A
Buxus sempervirens		●	●	●		●		●	●	●	●	●	●				E
Carpinus betulus	●	●	●	●	●	●	●			●	●	●	●			●	A
'Fastigiata'	●	●	●	●	●	●	●	●	●			●	●				A
Carya cordiformis	●	●	●	●			●	●									● A

● STRONGLY RECOMMENDED   ● RECOMMENDED   ● NOT RECOMMENDED

SPECIES/CULTIVAR	SOIL					SITE					SHELTER			FEATURES			
	Wet soils	Clay soils	Chalk soils	Dry sandy soils	Industrial spoils	Seaside	Exposed sites	Smoke and fumes	Small spaces	Roads and streets	Hedges	Screens	Shelter belts	Flowers	Fruit	Bark	Leaves
C. ovata		○	●	●			●										● A
C. tomentosa		○				●	○										● A
Castanea sativa	●	○		○		○	●	○						●	●		● A
Catalpa bignonioides		○	●	●	●	●		●	○					●	●		●
'Aurea'		○	●	●	●		○										○
C. × erubescens	○	●	●	●	●	●		●	○					●	●		●
Cercidiphyllum japonicum	●	●	●														● A
Cercis siliquastrum		●	○	○		○		●	●					●	○		
Corylus colurna	○	○	○	○			●	●		●							●
Crataegus crus-galli	○	○	○	○	●	●	●	●		○	●				●		● A
C. × grignonensis	○	●				●	●	●			●				○		
C. × lavallei	○	○	○	○	●	●	●	●		○	●			●	●		● A
C. monogyna	○	○	●	○	●	●	●	●		●	●		●	●	●		
C. oxyacantha	●	●	○			●	●	●		●				●			
C. × prunifolia	○	○	○			●	●	●		●	●				●		● A
Davidia involucrata	○	○	●					○		○				○			
var. *vilmoriniana*	○	○	●					○		○				○	●		
Eucalyptus gunnii	●	○	●	○		●	●	○					●	●		●	● E
E. niphophila	●	○		●		●	○	○					●		○		● E
E. nitens	●	○				●		●					●			●	● E
Euodia hupehensis		○	●	●		○	●	●		●				○	○		●
Fagus sylvatica			●	●	●	○	●	●			●	●	●				● A
'Dawyck'		○	●	●		○	●	●	●	○		●					● A
'Asplenifolia'		○	○			●	●	○									
'Pendula'		○	○			●											

● STRONGLY RECOMMENDED   ○ RECOMMENDED   ● NOT RECOMMENDED

SPECIES/CULTIVAR	SOIL					SITE					SHELTER			FEATURES			
	Wet soils	Clay soils	Chalk soils	Dry sandy soils	Industrial spoils	Seaside	Exposed sites	Smoke and fumes	Small spaces	Roads and streets	Hedges	Screens	Shelter belts	Flowers	Fruit	Bark	Leaves
'Purpurea'		●	○	○	●	○	●	●									●
'Zlatia'			○	●	●		●	●	●								● A
Fraxinus americana	○	○		○			○	●					●				● A
F. angustifolia		○	○			●	●	●	●				●				
F. excelsior	●	○	○			○	●	●					●				
F. ornus	●	○	○	●		●	●	●	●					○			
F. oxycarpa	○	○		●		○	○	○	○							●	●
'Raywood'	○	●	○	●		○	○	●		●						●	● A
Gleditsia triacanthos		○	○	●	●		●	●					●			●	● A
'Inermis'		●	○	●	●		●	●		●			●			●	● A
'Sunburst'		●	○	○	●		●	●	●								●
Griselinia littoralis	○	○				●	○										● E
Ilex × altaclarensis 'Camellifolia'	○	○	○	○		○	●	●			●	●				●	● E
'Golden King'	○	○		○		●	●	●			●	●				●	● E
'Hendersonii'	○	○		○		●	●	●			●	●					● E
'Hodginsii'	○	●		○		●	●	●			●	●					● E
I. aquifolium	○	●	●	●		●	●	●			○	●			●		E
'Bacciflava'	○	●	●	●		●	●	●			○				●		E
'Ferox'	○	●	●	○		●	●	●				●					● E
'Handsworth New Silver'	○	●	●	○		○	○	○									● E
'Perry's Weeping Holly'	○	●	●	○		●	●	●				●					● E
Juglans nigra	○	○	●					○								●	○
J. regia	○	○	○	○		○	○	○							○		
Koelreuteria paniculata		○	●	○		●	●			●			●	●			●

● STRONGLY RECOMMENDED　　　○ RECOMMENDED　　　● NOT RECOMMENDED

SPECIES/CULTIVAR	SOIL					SITE					SHELTER			FEATURES				
	Wet soils	Clay soils	Chalk soils	Dry sandy soils	Industrial spoils	Seaside	Exposed sites	Smoke and fumes	Small spaces	Roads and streets	Hedges	Screens	Shelter belts	Flowers	Fruit	Bark	Leaves	
Laurus nobilis		○	○	●		●	●	○			●	●	●		●		●	E
Ligustrum lucidum		○	○			●	●	●	○		●		●	○			●	E
Liquidambar formosana var. *monticola*	○	●	●	●		●	●	●									●	A
L. styraciflua	●	●	●	●		○	●	●	●								●	A
Liriodendron chinense	●	●	○	○		●		●	●					○			●	A
L. tulipifera	○	●	○	○		●	●	●						●			●	A
'Aureomarginatum'	○	●	○	●													●	
'Fastigiatum'	○	●	○	●		●	●	●	○	●							●	A
Magnolia campbellii	○	●		○		●	●	○						○				
'Charles Raffill'	○	●		○		●	●	○						○				
M. denudata	○	●	●	○		●	●	○						●				
M. grandiflora 'Goliath'	○	○	●	●		○		●	●					○			●	E
M. salicifolia	○	○	●											○				
Malus × *atrosanguinea*	●	●	○	○		●	○	○		●				○				
M. floribunda		●	○		●	●	●	○		●				○				
M. 'Golden Hornet'	●	●	○	○	●	○	○	○						●	○			
M. hupehensis	●	●	○	○	●	●	●	●		●		●		●	●			
M 'John Downie'	●	●	○	○		○	○	○		●				○	○			
M. × *purpurea*	●	●	○	○	●	○	○	●		●				○	●			
M. tschonoskii	●	○	○	●	●		●		○			●					●	A
Nothofagus dombeyi	●		○					●				●					○	E
N. obliqua	○	○	●	○			●	●					●				●	A
N. procera		●	○	●			●	●					●				●	A
Nyssa sylvatica	○	●															○	A
Paulownia tomentosa		○	○	○		○	●	○		●				●			●	

● STRONGLY RECOMMENDED ○ RECOMMENDED ● NOT RECOMMENDED

53

SPECIES/CULTIVAR	SOIL					SITE					SHELTER			FEATURES				
	Wet soils	Clay soils	Chalk soils	Dry sandy soils	Industrial spoils	Seaside	Exposed sites	Smoke and fumes	Small spaces	Roads and streets	Hedges	Screens	Shelter belts	Flowers	Fruit	Bark	Leaves	
Platanus × acerifolia	●	●	●	●	●	●	●	●		●						●	●	
'Suttneri'	●	●	●	●		●	●	●		●							●	
P. orientalis	●	●	●	●		●	●	●		●						●	●	A
Populus alba	●	●	●	●		●	●	●				●	●			●	●	
'Racket'	●	●	●	●	●	●	●	●	●	●							●	
'Richardii'	●	●	●	●		●	●	●	●								●	
P. candicans 'Aurora'	●	●	●	●	●	●	●	●									●	
P. canescens	●	●	●	●		●	●	●					●			●	●	
P. × euramericana 'Eugenei'	●	●	●	●	●		●				●							
'Robusta'	●	●	●	●	●	●	●	●			●				●			
'Serotina'	●	●	●	●	●	●	●	●			●							
'Serotina Aurea'	●	●	●	●		●	●	●			●						●	
P. nigra var. betulifolia	●	●	●	●	●	●	●	●			●							
'Gigantea'	●	●	●	●		●	●	●	●		●							
'Italica'	●	●	●	●		●	●	●	●		●							
'Vereecken'	●	●	●	●		●	●	●	●		●							
P. trichocarpa and cultivars	●	●		●	●	●	●	●				●	●				●	
'Balsam Spire'	●	●		●	●	●	●	●			●							
Prunus avium		●	●	●		●	●	●		●			●	●	●			A
'Plena'		●	●	●		●	●	●		●				●				A
P. dulcis	●	●	●	●		●	●	●		●				●				
P. maackii	●	●	●	●		●	●	●								●		
P. padus	●	●	●	●			●	●						●				
'Watereri'	●	●	●	●		●	●	●						●				

● STRONGLY RECOMMENDED   ● RECOMMENDED   ● NOT RECOMMENDED

SPECIES/CULTIVAR	SOIL					SITE					SHELTER			FEATURES			
	Wet soils	Clay soils	Chalk soils	Dry sandy soils	Industrial spoils	Seaside	Exposed sites	Smoke and fumes	Small spaces	Roads and streets	Hedges	Screens	Shelter belts	Flowers	Fruit	Bark	Leaves
P. sargentii[1]	○	○	○	○		○	○	●		●				○			A
'Kursar'	●	○	○	●		●		●	●	●				○			
'Shosar'		○	○	●		●		●	●	●				●			
P. serrula	○	○	○	○		●	●	○						●		●	
P. 'Amanogawa'	●	○	○	●		●		●	●	○				●			A
P. 'Fugenzo'	●	○	○	●		●	●							●			
P. 'Hokusai'	●	○	○	○		○	○	○	●					○			A
P. 'Horinji'	●	○	○	●		●		●		●				●			
P. 'Kanzan'	●	○	○	○		○	○	●		○				●			A
P. 'Kiku-shidare'	●	○	○	●		●	●	●						○			
P. 'Okiku'	●	○	○	●		●		●		●				●			
P. 'Pink Perfection'	○	○	●	○		○	●	●		○				●			
P. 'Shimidsu'	●	○	○	○		○	○	●						●			
P. 'Shirofugen'	●	○	○	●		○	○	●						●			
P. 'Shirotae'	●	○	○	●		●	●							●			
P. 'Tai-haku'	●	○	○	○		●	●	●		○				●		●	A
P. 'Ukon'	●	○	○	○		●	●	●		○				●			
P. subhirtella 'Autumnalis'	○	○	○	○		○	○	●						○			
'Pendula'	●	○	○	○		○	○							○			
P. × yedoensis	○	○	○	○		●	●	○		●				●			
Pterocarya fraxinifolia	●	●	○	●			●	○							●		A
P. × rehderana	●	○	○	○			●	○							●		A
Pyrus calleryana 'Bradford'	○	●	○	○		●	○	●	○	●		●	●				

[1]Ornamental cherries normally on *P. avium* rootstock; affected by soils in same manner.

● STRONGLY RECOMMENDED   ○ RECOMMENDED   ● NOT RECOMMENDED

SPECIES/CULTIVAR	SOIL					SITE					SHELTER			FEATURES			
	Wet soils	Clay soils	Chalk soils	Dry sandy soils	Industrial spoils	Seaside	Exposed sites	Smoke and fumes	Small spaces	Roads and streets	Hedges	Screens	Shelter belts	Flowers	Fruit	Bark	Leaves
'Chanticleer'	●	●	●	○		●	○	●	○	●				○			● A
P. salicifolia		●	○	○		●	●	○	○					●			●
Quercus acutissima	●	●		●		●		●		●							●
Q. canariensis	○	○	○	○		○											●
Q. castaneifolia		●	○	○		○		○									●
Q. cerris	○	○	●	○		●	○	●				●	●				
Q. coccinea	○	●		○				○					●				● A
Q. frainetto	○	○	●	○		○	●										●
Q. × hispanica 'Lucombeana'	○	○	○	○		●	○	○				●	●				● E
Q. ilex	●	●	●	○		●	●	●			●	●	●				E
Q. macranthera	○	●		○		○	○					●	●				●
Q. palustris	○	●		○				○		○		●	●				● A
Q. petraea	●	●	●	●	●	●	●	●									●
Q. phellos	○	●		○		○	●	●	○								●
Q. robur	○	●	●	●	●	○	●	○				●	●				● A
'Concordia'	●	●	○	○													● A
'Fastigiata'	○	●	●	○	●	○	○		●			●					○ A
Q. rubra	○	○	○	○	○	●	●	●		●							● A
Robinia pseudoacacia		○	●	●	○	○	●	●		●				●			
'Frisia'		○	○	○	○			●	○	●				●			○
Salix alba	●	●	●	○		○	○	●				●				●	●
'Chermesina'	●	●	●	●		●	○	●				●	●			●	
'Coerulea'	●	●	●	●		●	●	○				●					
'Tristis'	●	●	●	○		○	○	●				●					
S. caprea	●	○		○	●	○	●					●		●			

● STRONGLY RECOMMENDED   ○ RECOMMENDED   ● NOT RECOMMENDED

SPECIES/CULTIVAR	Wet soils	Clay soils	Chalk soils	Dry sandy soils	Industrial spoils	Seaside	Exposed sites	Smoke and fumes	Small spaces	Roads and streets	Hedges	Screens	Shelter belts	Flowers	Fruit	Bark	Leaves
S. daphnoides	●	●	○	●	●	○	○	●			●					●	●
S. fragilis	●	●	●		○	●	○	●			●						
S. matsudana 'Tortuosa'	●	●	○	○		●	●	●									
S. pentandra	●	●		●		●	○	●					●				●
Sorbus aria		●	●	●	●	○	●	●		●			●	●	●		● A
'Chrysophylla'		●	●	●			○	○									
Decaisneana		●	●	○		●	○	●			○	○		○	○	●	A
'Lutescens'		●	●	●		●	●	○	●		●	●		○	○		● A
S. aucuparia	●	●	○	●	●	●	●	●		○		●	●	○	○	○	●
'Beissneri'		●	○	●		●	○	●		○					●	●	● A
'Xanthocarpa'		○	○	○		○	○	○		○			●	○	○		
S. cashmiriana	●	●	●	●		○	○	○						●	●		
S. cuspidata	●	○	○			●	●	○						○	○		○
S. domestica		○		○			○	○		●				●	●		
S. commixta 'Embley'	○	●	●	○		●	●	●		●				○	○		● A
S. hupehensis	●	○	●	●		○	○	○		●				○	○		●
S. intermedia		●	●	●		●	●	●		●				●	●		●
S. 'Joseph Rock'		●	●	○		○	○	●	●	●				●	●		● A
S. sargentiana		●	●	○		●	●	●		○				●	○		● A
S. thibetica 'John Mitchell'	○	●	●	○			○		○					○	●		●
S. torminalis	○	●	○	○			○			●							● A
S. 'Wilfrid Fox'		●	○	○		○	●	●		●				●	○		●
Tilia cordata	○	○	○	○	●		●	●			○	○		○			
T. euchlora		●	○	○	●	○	○	●		○	●	●					●
T. mongolica		●	●	●		○	○	●		○							●
T. petiolaris		●	●	●		●	○	●		●							●

● STRONGLY RECOMMENDED   ○ RECOMMENDED   ● NOT RECOMMENDED

SPECIES/CULTIVAR	SOIL					SITE					SHELTER			FEATURES			
	Wet soils	Clay soils	Chalk soils	Dry sandy soils	Industrial spoils	Seaside	Exposed sites	Smoke and fumes	Small spaces	Roads and streets	Hedges	Screens	Shelter belts	Flowers	Fruit	Bark	Leaves
T. platyphyllos	●	●	●	●	●	●	●	●		●							
'Rubra'	●	●	●	●	●	●	●	●		●						●	
T. tomentosa	●	●	●	●		●	●	●		●			●	●			●
Ulmus carpinifolia		●	●		●	●	●	●		●							A
var. cornubiensis		●	●			●	●	●	●	●	●						A
var. sarniensis		●	●	●	●	●	●	●	●	●	●						A
U. glabra	●	●	●			●	●	●			●	●					
'Camperdown'	●	●	●			●		●	●								
'Lutescens'	●	●	●			●		●		●							
U. × hollandica 'Vegeta'		●	●	●		●	●			●	●	●		●			
U. parvifolia	●	●	●	●		●	●	●								●	●
U. pumila	●	●		●		●	●	●									●
Zelkova carpinifolia		●	●	●			●	●									A
Z. serrata		●	●	●			●	●		●	●	●				●	● A
Z. sinica		●	●	●			●	●		●							
CONIFERS																	
Abies alba	●	●		●		●	●										
A. bracteata		●	●														
A. cephalonica	●	●	●	●		●	●										
A. concolor	●	●															
var. lowiana	●	●		●		●	●										
'Violacea'	●	●		●					●								
A. grandis	●	●				●	●										
A. homolepis	●	●		●		●	●										
A. nordmanniana	●	●						●									

● STRONGLY RECOMMENDED   ● RECOMMENDED   ● NOT RECOMMENDED

SPECIES/CULTIVAR	SOIL					SITE					SHELTER			FEATURES			
	Wet soils	Clay soils	Chalk soils	Dry sandy soils	Industrial spoils	Seaside	Exposed sites	Smoke and fumes	Small spaces	Roads and streets	Hedges	Screens	Shelter belts	Flowers	Fruit	Bark	Leaves
A. numidica	◐	●		●		◐	◐	●									
A. procera	◐	●		◐			●										●
A. veitchii	◐	◐		●			●										
Araucaria araucana	●	●	●	●		◐	●										
Cedrus atlantica	◐	●	●	●		◐	◐	◐									
var. *glauca*	◐	●	●	●		◐	◐	◐									◐
C. deodara	◐	◐	◐	◐			◐	◐									
C. libani	◐	●	●	●		●	●	◐									
Chamaecyparis lawsoniana	●	●	●	◐	●	●	●	●	◐		●	●	●				
'Allumii'	●	●	●	◐	●	●	●	●	●		●	●	●				●
'Columnaris'	●	●	●	◐		●	●	●	◐								●
'Ellwoodii'	●	●	●	◐		●	●	●	◐		●						
'Fletcheri'	●	●	●	◐		●	●	●	●		●	●					●
'Green Pillar'	●	●	●	◐		●	●	◐	●		●	●					●
'Green Spire'	●	●	●	◐		●	●	●	●			●					●
'Hillieri'	●	●	●	◐		●	◐	●									
'Lutea'	●	●	●	●	●	◐	◐	◐	◐			●	●				●
'Lanei'	●	●	●	◐		●	◐	●	◐								●
'Pottenii'	●	●	●	◐		●	●	●	◐								
'Stewartii'	●	●	●	◐		●	●	●	●			●	●				●
'Triomphe de Boskoop'	●	●	●	◐		●	●	●	◐			●	●				●
'Winston Churchill'	●	●	●	◐		●	●	●	●								●
'Wisselii'	●	●	●	◐		●	●	●	●								
C. nootkatensis	◐	●	◐	◐		◐	●	●	●								
C. obtusa	◐	●															

● STRONGLY RECOMMENDED   ◐ RECOMMENDED   ● NOT RECOMMENDED

SPECIES/CULTIVAR	SOIL					SITE					SHELTER			FEATURES			
	Wet soils	Clay soils	Chalk soils	Dry sandy soils	Industrial spoils	Seaside	Exposed sites	Smoke and fumes	Small spaces	Roads and streets	Hedges	Screens	Shelter belts	Flowers	Fruit	Bark	Leaves
'Crippsii'	○	●	○	●		○	○	○					●				●
C. pisifera	○	●		○		●	○	○									●
'Aurea'	○	○		○		●											●
'Filifera Aurea'		●		●		○			●								●
'Plumosa'		●	○	●		○		○									
'Plumosa Aurea'		●	○	●		○		○									●
'Squarrosa'		●	○	●		○		●									
Cryptomeria japonica	●	●	●	○		○	○	○			●						
'Elegans'	○	●	●	○		●											
'Lobbii'	●	●	●	○		●	○	●									
× Cupressocyparis leylandii	○	○	○	○	○	●	●	○			●	●	●				
'Castlewellen Gold'	○	●	○	○	●	●	●	○				○	○				○
'Haggerston Grey'	○	●	○	○		●	●	○			●	○					
'Leighton Green'	○	●	○	○	○	●	●	○			●	●	●				
'Naylor's Blue'	○	●	○	○			●	●	●		●	●					●
'Robinson's Gold'		●	○	○													○
'Stapehill 20'	●	●	○			●	●	●									
'Stapehill 21'	○	●	○	○	●		○	○			●	●	●				
Cupressus glabra	●	●	●	●		○	○	●	●		○	○	○				●
'Pyramidalis'		●	●	●		○	○	●				○	●				●
C. lusitanica	○			○		●											
var. benthamii	●	○		●													
'Glauca'	●	○		●													●
C. macrocarpa	○	○	○	○		●	○	●				○	○				
'Donard Gold'	●	●	○	○		●											●

● STRONGLY RECOMMENDED   ○ RECOMMENDED   ● NOT RECOMMENDED

SPECIES/CULTIVAR	SOIL					SITE					SHELTER			FEATURES			
	Wet soils	Clay soils	Chalk soils	Dry sandy soils	Industrial spoils	Seaside	Exposed sites	Smoke and fumes	Small spaces	Roads and streets	Hedges	Screens	Shelter belts	Flowers	Fruit	Bark	Leaves
'Lutea'	●	●	●	●		●	●	●									●
C. torulosa	●	●					●										
Ginkgo biloba	●	●	●	●	●	●	●	●	●	●							● AD
'Fastigiata'	●	●	●	●	●	●	●	●	●	●							● AD
Juniperus drupacea		●	●	●					●								
Larix decidua	●	●	●	●	●	●	●	●				●	●				● AD
L. × eurolepis	●	●	●	●	●	●	●	●				●	●				● AD
L. kaempferi	●	●	●	●	●	●	●	●				●	●				● AD
Metasequoia glyptostroboides	●	●	●	●				●	●							●	● AD
Picea abies	●	●		●	●		●				●						
P. brewerana	●	●	●					●									
P. omorika	●	●	●	●			●	●	●			●					
P. orientalis	●	●	●	●			●										
'Aurea'	●	●	●	●													
P. pungens var. glauca	●	●		●		●	●	●									●
P. sitchensis	●	●			●	●	●	●				●					
Pinus ayacahuite		●		●		●	●	●							●		
P. cembra	●	●	●	●		●	●	●	●								
P. contorta var. contorta	●	●		●	●	●	●	●				●					
P. jeffreyi		●		●			●								●		
P. leucodermis	●	●	●	●		●	●	●	●						●		
P. muricata	●	●		●		●	●	●				●					
P. nigra var. maritima	●	●	●	●	●	●	●	●				●					
var. nigra		●	●	●	●	●	●	●				●					
P. peuce	●	●	●	●	●	●	●	●									
P. pinaster			●			●	●	●				●			●	●	

● STRONGLY RECOMMENDED   ● RECOMMENDED   ● NOT RECOMMENDED

SPECIES/CULTIVAR	SOIL					SITE					SHELTER			FEATURES			
	Wet soils	Clay soils	Chalk soils	Dry sandy soils	Industrial spoils	Seaside	Exposed sites	Smoke and fumes	Small spaces	Roads and streets	Hedges	Screens	Shelter belts	Flowers	Fruit	Bark	Leaves
P. ponderosa		●	●			●	○									●	
P. radiata	●	○		●	●	●	○					●	●	●			
P. sylvestris		●		●	○		●	●			●		●			●	
P. wallichiana	●	●	●	○				●							○		●
Podocarpus andinus	●	●		○		●	●	●			○						
Pseudotsuga menziesii	○	○		●		●											
var. glauca	●	○		○													
Sequoia sempervirens	●	○		●								●				●	
Sequoiadendron giganteum	○	○	●	○		○	●	●					●				
Taxodium distichum	●	●	●			●	●	●		●							● AD
Taxus baccata	○	○	●	○		●	●	●			●	●	●				
'Adpressa'	○	○	●	○		○	○	●	●								
'Dovastoniana'	○	○	●	○		●											
'Fastigiata'	○	○	●	○		○	●	○	●								
Thuja occidentalis	●	●	○	●		●	●	○			●	●	●				
'Lutea'	●	●	○	●		●	●										●
'Spiralis'	●	●	○	●		●			○								
T. orientalis	○		●	○		●	●	●			●						
'Elegantissima'	○		●	○		●			○								●
T. plicata	●	○	○	○		●	○				○	●	●				
'Semperaurescens'	●	●	○	●		●	●										●
'Zebrina'	●	○	○	●		●	●				●	●					●
Thujopsis dolabrata	●	●	○	●		●							●				●
Tsuga canadensis	●	●		○		●	○				●	●	●				
T. caroliniana	○	○															●
T. heterophylla	●	●		●		○	●				●	●	●				
T. mertensiana	○	●		●		○	●		●								●

● STRONGLY RECOMMENDED   ○ RECOMMENDED   ● NOT RECOMMENDED

38400

PLATE 22
In this development at Washington
New Town, woodland trees, street
trees and garden trees are all
components in a successful design.

38395

PLATE 23
Without trees this scene would be
bleak indeed.

38761

38302

PLATE 24
Main shopping mall, Milton Keynes.

PLATE 25
These trees have outlived their purpose
and before long their removal will
prove costly and difficult.

64

Design

At the design stage selection will be made from this list of suitable species and decisions will be made on the basis of the site requirements of the trees (will the trees grow easily and with minimum maintenance on the chosen site?). The cost and availability of suitable species and cultivars will need to be considered together with a careful look at any disadvantages which may arise in future management; for instance common lime trees may look fine in a car park, but the honeydew exuded by aphids on these trees will cause problems with motorists because of the sticky secretion deposited on cars parked under the trees' shade.

It is particularly important that designers at this stage should consult with foresters and arboriculturists in order to make certain that the trees they have chosen will actually thrive and have no undesirable secondary characteristics.

Operation plan

The implementation of the design may require an operation plan describing the sequence of operations from procurement of suitable planting stock, site preparation, delivery and handling of trees and the planting operation, through to weed control and aftercare. In drawing up this plan the characteristics and needs of the species chosen must be kept in mind. For example most evergreens are best planted from late winter to early spring in order to reduce the amount of time the disturbed tree is exposed to the cold desiccating winds of winter; conversely most deciduous species are best planted late in the year as soon as autumn frosts have caused them to harden off.

Management plan

A management plan which can provide the basis for care of the trees throughout their lives need not be a weighty document. It is often best kept in the form of a statement of objectives together with the original design, a copy of the operation plan and proposals for future action. A management plan should describe briefly the regular maintenance operations which are envisaged. It should also record action taken.

If the choice of species has been wise so that the trees are at home on the site, are growing to the size and shape envisaged and are not in conflict with other features of the development, then regular maintenance should be simple and not costly.

A management plan will need to take account of the characteristics of the species chosen and it might, for example, call for the early removal of a fast growing component species which was deliberately chosen to provide a quick screen for early shelter or to nurse a slower growing species during the early years of the scheme. It should be noted that the management of existing trees and the use of natural regeneration require just as much attention as new plantings and a management plan in such situations should have regard to the characteristics of the trees found on the site. For example, heavy shade bearing species such as beech or sycamore will soon come to dominate all other vegetation unless specific plans are made to thin in order to maintain light levels suitable for light demanding species.

Appropriate trees

When considering the choice of species or cultivars in a wide range of situations from near rural, peri-urban locations at one extreme to city centre development at the other, it is a good plan to consider a group of closely related or similar trees with desirable characteristics and then to select from this group species and cultivars especially suited to specific locations. As a rule of thumb it can be said that familiar (often native or naturalised) species will be appropriate in the rural fringe, while the increasingly striking characteristics that can be found in cultivars and exotics will become appropriate as the environment becomes more and more man-made. A selection of trees appropriate to specific purposes and locations is given in Table 6.2.

The birches – an example of species choice

The different features which can be found in a group of related trees may be illustrated by the genus *Betula* – the birches. These trees are of particular value in urban forestry. Birches tolerate a wide range of soils including chalk, sand and clay and they will survive in exposed positions. They are attractive at all times of the year, grow quickly when young but never become massive and the leaves present hardly any problems in autumn. This attractive group of trees offers species and cultivars for almost

Table 6.2 Choosing the tree for the site: examples of tree selection based on purpose and location

Species with potential for timber production/firewood, shelter or wildlife conservation. Suitable for urban fringe woodlands, large parks and roadsides.	Trees suitable for suburban developments, recreation areas, small parks and streets.	Small decorative cultivars and exotics with colours and shapes that provide year-round interest; suitable for city centre developments, office blocks and formal gardens.
BROADLEAVES		
Alders		
Alnus cordata	*Alnus glutinosa* 'Aurea'	*Alnus incana* 'Pendula' or 'Imperialis'
Alnus glutinosa		
Ash		
Fraxinus excelsior	*Fraxinus excelsior* 'Pendula'	*Fraxinus oxycarpa* 'Raywood'
	Fraxinus ornus	
Beech		
Fagus sylvatica	*Fagus sylvatica* 'Dawyck'	*Fagus sylvatica* 'Aurea pendula'
Birches		
Betula pendula	*Betula pendula* 'Dalecarlica'	*Betula pendula* 'Youngii'
	Betula jacquemontii	
Cherries		
Prunus avium	*Prunus avium* 'Plena'	A huge range of Japanese ornamental flowering cherries is available
	Prunus subhirtella	
'Chestnuts'		
Castanea sativa	*Aesculus indica*	*Aesculus parviflora*
Elms		
None recommended in view of Dutch elm disease		

Species with potential for timber production/firewood, shelter or wildlife conservation. Suitable for urban fringe woodlands, large parks and roadsides.	Trees suitable for suburban developments, recreation areas, small parks and streets.	Small decorative cultivars and exotics with colours and shapes that provide year-round interest; suitable for city centre developments, office blocks and formal gardens.
Hazel *Corylus avellana* *Corylus colurna*	*Corylus maxima* 'Purpurea'	*Corylus avellana* 'Contorta'
Laurels None	*Prunus laurocerasus* *Prunus lusitanica*	None
Maples and Planes *Acer campestre* *Acer pseudoplatanus* *Platanus* × *hispanica* (London plane)	*Acer platanoides* 'Drummondii' or 'Schwedleri'	*Acer capillipes* *Acer palmatum* 'Dissectum'
Oak *Quercus petraea* *Quercus robur*	*Quercus rubra* 'Aurea'	None recommended
Poplars *Populus alba* *Populus nigra* *Populus tremula*	None recommended and should not be planted near buildings	
Rowan and Whitebeam *Sorbus aucuparia*	*Sorbus hupehensis* *Sorbus aria*	*Sorbus aucuparia* 'Beissneri' *Sorbus sargentii* *Sorbus aria* 'Pendula'
Thorns *Crataegus monogyna*	*Crataegus* × *prunifolia*	*Crataegus oxyacantha* 'Paul's Scarlet'
Willows *Salix alba*	*Salix alba* 'Vitellina'	*Salix caprea* 'Kilmarnock' *Salix daphnoides*

Species with potential for timber production/firewood, shelter or wildlife conservation. Suitable for urban fringe woodlands, large parks and roadsides.	Trees suitable for suburban developments, recreation areas, small parks and streets.	Small decorative cultivars and exotics with colours and shapes that provide year-round interest; suitable for city centre developments, office blocks and formal gardens.

CONIFERS

Cedars and Cypresses

Thuja plicata × *Cupressocyparis leylandii*	*Cedrus atlantica* 'Glauca' *Chamaecyparis lawsoniana* 'Stewartii'	*Chamaecyparis lawsoniana* 'Allumii' or 'Columnaris'

Firs

Pseudotsuga menziesii *Abies grandis* *Abies nobilis*	*Abies pinsapo*	*Abies koreana*

Junipers

None	*Juniperus communis* *Juniperus drupaceae*	Many cultivars, e.g. 'Skyrocket', 'Pfitzerana'

Pines

Pinus nigra *Pinus sylvestris*	*Pinus parviflora*	*Pinus densiflora* 'Pendula'

Spruces

Picea abies *Picea sitchensis*	*Picea breweriana*	*Picea abies* 'Inversa'

PLATE 26
Betula pendula.

PLATE 27
Betula pendula 'Dalecarlica'.

PLATE 28
Betula jacquemontii.

PLATE 29
Betula jacquemontii, close-up of bark.

all urban situations, but the choice should reflect the surroundings in a scheme and the indiscriminate use of only one species, *Betula pendula*, in the past, together with its tendency to regenerate freely on old heathland sites, have led many people to regard birch as little more than a weed. *Betula pendula* is nevertheless the appropriate choice on the urban fringe, in villages and in other locations where the background has a significant rural component. Our other native birch *Betula pubescens* also has a place in difficult boggy conditions as it will tolerate cold wet soils.

Plantings in the larger towns and suburbs of cities can take advantage of the more graceful characteristics of the Swedish birch, *Betula pendula* 'Dalecarlica', a northern variant of our own silver birch. In the extremely formal surroundings of city centre developments the striking appearance of species such as *Betula jacquemontii*, *Betula papyrifera* and *Betula albo-sinensis* 'Septentrionalis' will ensure that these trees are significant features throughout the year.

None of the birches becomes a very large tree, so problems with scale are seldom encountered with this genus. Taking scale into account is however important with trees which in their normal form would grow too large in most urban surroundings.

A similar approach to that outlined above can be adopted in most situations, with increasing attention to the smaller or slower growing species and cultivars as one progresses from rural to city centre conditions.

Table 6.2 contains many examples of these principles, which can help to avoid the frequent problem of trees that look incongruous in their surroundings.

7 The planting stock

The conventional practice in planting is to use seedlings and transplants raised in nurseries. The alternative of sowing seed at the site is rare in urban forestry. This is because many seeds are usually needed to guarantee that at least one tree survives where it is wanted, since so many hazards face both seed and the newly germinating seedling which are difficult to control out in the open. It is easier and safer to achieve a satisfactory stocking of trees by raising them in the protected environment of the nursery and then planting on site. An exception is natural regeneration of species which sets seed frequently and heavily, such as ash, sycamore, birch and sallow but only occasionally will these be of value in urban forestry apart from areas in or near existing woodland.

Planning ahead

Many types and sizes of planting stock are available from the nursery trade – these are described in British Standard 3936. Just as one tree species is not suited to every site so reliance on one stock type for all planting is unlikely to satisfy the many objectives of urban forestry and achieve economical establishment and good growth. Discrimination is needed to match stock type to requirements, and this requires careful planning. Also it is easy to waste money, such as planting large numbers of expensive standards, when planting smaller and cheaper trees would have been far better.

Since all types of trees should be planted while they are dormant, either in the autumn or early spring (unless mild, the period from Christmas to mid-February is best avoided), it is desirable to place orders for plants in the summer before planting. The beginning of the planning cycle – deciding species, plant types, numbers, etc. – should start at the latest in the previous spring.

Types of planting stock

Four quite distinct types of planting stock need to be recognised:

1. bare root or open grown – plants lifted from the nursery soil and despatched to the planting site with roots bare of soil;
2. container grown plants – plants with a ball of soil attached to the roots and usually grown in a container;
3. root balled plants – field grown plants which are lifted with soil attached to the roots and the root ball wrapped with hessian or similar material;
4. sets – woody shoots of species such as poplars and willows which will root easily when inserted into the soil.

Bare root plants

In the winter, while trees are dormant, plants can be safely lifted from the nursery, soil gently shaken from their roots, packaged, transported and successfully planted at the new site even if hundreds of miles away. Provided care is taken to prevent desiccation or overheating, several weeks can elapse between lifting plants from the nursery and finally planting them without any harm being suffered.

For these reasons, and for convenience of handling large numbers, most trees planted in Great Britain are bare root stock. Provided such plants are carefully handled, protected from drying out and planted at the proper time, use of bare root stock is both safe and economical. In general such stock should receive first consideration.

Container grown plants

Plants bought from garden centres and amenity tree nurseries are mostly in containers to improve presentation and facilitate out-of-season planting. However, it should be noted that they generally confer no other advantages and may even inadvertently encourage poor handling and bad planting practices.

Numerous types of container exist – clay and polythene pots, paper cells, shaped plastic modules, pre-formed trays, etc. – but all are simply receptacles to hold a growing medium in which the plant develops. All containers must be removed before planting; even truly degradable ones designed to break down in the soil can inhibit root development.

The size of container is, or at least should be, dictated by the ultimate size of plants to be grown in them. Large plants must have large soil volumes and hence large containers in which to grow.

Container grown plants have four disadvantages:

1. plants grown for too long in a container become 'pot bound', i.e. their roots begin to spiral around the container and when finally planted will initiate few if any new outward growing roots;

2. they are bulky to transport since soil is carried from the nursery to the planting site;

3. because plants are in a growing medium there is a temptation to neglect them or keep them too long in the container, so leading to delayed planting or unbalanced growth (e.g. much top growth on a small root), both of which reduce survival;

4. they are generally more expensive than bare root plants of similar size.

The one advantage container plants appear to offer, namely of being plantable during the growing season, is not in practice a benefit. Despite having a root ball, survival is still poorer than conventional winter planting and the cost of container plants is, size for size, always higher than bare root ones.

Root balled plants

Many evergreens and some large broadleaves are available in this form. While minimising root disturbance they are bulky to transport. The wrapping should be removed at planting. As with container grown plants there may be an initial tendency for new roots to grow only in the accompanying root ball rather than establish in the soil of the planting site, especially if that soil is less hospitable.

Sets

Poplars and willows can be planted using sets. These are sticks, usually 1 or 2-year-old shoots between 2 and 3 metres long, which are inserted into the ground to a depth of up to one metre. It is possible on well cultivated ground to use short sets about 25 cm long. Sets should never be pushed into soil but inserted into a hole made with a crowbar and the slight space around the set filled with sand or similar friable medium. Using sets is a simple and inexpensive way of establishing trees of these species.

Size of plants

In many urban forestry plantings, because of the importance of amenity, immediate visual impact is considered to be important. In conventional forestry all effort can be directed towards ensuring good survival and growth at minimum cost; in urban forestry good appearance must often be added to these other criteria. This creates a dilemma. Large plants, such as heavy standards perhaps 3 or 4 metres tall, which provide the immediate visual effect, are not only very expensive but also by far the hardest to establish and get growing well. As stressed earlier, forward planning of new developments can alleviate this difficulty by providing for establishment of small trees well in advance. However, in practice this frequently does not happen and recourse is made to planting large trees, all too often with disappointing results.

Three main sizes of tree are offered by nurserymen though there are many subdivisions within each category. Table 7.1 summarises specifications recommended in BS 3936:1980.

Seedlings, transplants and undercuts

These are small trees less than 1.2 m tall which may be up to 3 or 4 years old. Seedlings are plants which have not been moved from the place where they were sown (nursery bed or container) while transplants, as the name implies, have been moved from one nursery bed to another to improve root development. Sometimes instead of physically moving the plants they are undercut in the bed where they are growing to sever downward growing and lateral roots. In trade catalogues these categories can be identified as follows:

seedlings	1+0, 2+0;
transplants	1+1, 2+1, 1+1+1, etc.;
undercuts	lul, lulul.

In the above notation the '1' refers to the year(s) the plant was

Table 7.1   Dimensions of trees according to designation

Designation	Circumference of stem 1 m above ground (cm)	Minimum height (m)	Maximum height (m)	Clear stem height to lowest branch (m)
Seedling	–	–	–	–
Transplant	–	–	1.20	–
Whip	–	1.20	2.50	–
Feathered	–	1.80	3.00	–
Half standard	–	1.80	2.10	1.20–1.50
Standard	8–10	2.75	3.00	1.80 (min.)
Heavy standard (tall and selected grades)	8–12	3.00	3.50	1.80 (min.)

Modified from Tables 1 and 2 in BS 3936: Part 1: 1980.

grown, the '+' indicates lifting from one bed to another, i.e. transplanting, the 'u' indicates undercutting, e.g. a 2+1 is a plant which grew for 2 years in the seedbed and then was transplanted and allowed to grow on for 1 year. Sometimes fast growing species such as cherry (*Prunus*) may be undercut or even moved in mid season which is shown as a ½, e.g. ½+½.

In general the longer the plants have been grown in the nursery the more expensive they will be: prices in 1989 typically range from 15 to 50 pence per plant.

Transplants, typically 1+1, are the stock-in-trade of conventional forestry planting. They are the recommended plant type for the great bulk of urban forestry plantings where groups or blocks of trees are intended since, with proper treatment, they establish quickly and begin to make rapid growth often in the first year after planting.

Whips

Whips are taller plants between 1.2 and 1.5 metres and usually 4–5 or more years old. Where they are furnished with branches all along the stem they may be termed 'feathered' whips. Being larger and older plants whips are more expensive, typically costing between £1 and £2 each. Their use should be confined to single line plantings next to walls or fences and occasionally small groups in corners of parks or fields. Block plantings designed to give woodland effect should be carried out using transplants.

Half standards, standards and heavy standards

These are large plant sizes which will normally have been pruned to give a branch-free stem to 1.5 m and have a branched head. Specifications are shown in Table 7.1. Again depending on species, size and age, they may cost up to £50 each but clearly, owing to their size, will give some immediate effect. Even with the most careful planting, however, newly planted standards rarely look healthy in the first 1 or 2 years in the field. Typically leaves tend to be small, some shoots die back and the crown looks thin. Ample watering in the first year will help to alleviate these problems on dry soils but worsen them on wet, compacted, poorly draining ones and obviously add further to the expense.

Mass plantings of such trees, i.e. groups of 10 or more, are difficult to justify. Their main use should be confined to spaced plantings in streets and shopping malls. However, use of ones or twos next to other plantings for landscape effect or in parkland where vandalism is expected may be worth trying but, as with all planting, every care must be taken to ensure satisfactory establishment of this costly plant type. Large trees need as much care and aftercare during establishment as small ones.

Semi-mature trees

These large trees are only exceptionally used for a single, very special planting. They have no place in urban forestry in general.

Comparative performance of different plant sizes.

The high cost of large plants has been stressed as an obvious disadvantage but poor post-planting performance underlines their unsuitability for widespread use as a cost effective technique; Figure 7.1 illustrates this. There is nothing more unsightly than sick, damaged standards supported by the woodwork of ugly stakes; there is nothing more pleasing than groups of vigorously growing young plants developing in balance with their new environment.

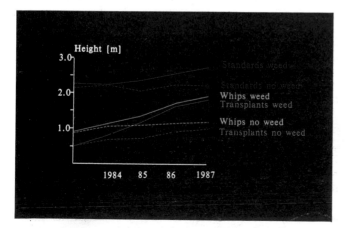

FIGURE 7.1
Height of rowan transplants, whips and standards with and without weed control.

Quality and health

Three important aspects of plant quality should be ascertained:

1. where did the seed or cultivar come from?
2. is physical or mechanical damage, disease or pest present?
3. is the plant sturdy rather than spindly, with a good balance between shoot and root?

Seed source

It is important to know the shape and size of tree the young plant will develop into. Many ornamental species and cultivars are regulated by Plant Breeders' Rights, the National Council for Conservation of Plants and Gardens (NCCPG) and the Institute of Horticultural Research, and standard sources of stock types are used. For forest trees, apart from oak and beech, such information is less precise and greater variation can be expected in the way the tree may develop in terms of habit, stem form, etc. The nurseryman should have information about where his seed or cutting material came from.

Appearance

Planting stock quality is usually judged by appearance: damage to roots, shoots and buds, evidence of fungal growth or insect pests, and scarred bark all indicate poor quality and possibly ill-health. The balance between root and shoot is also important; all plants should be furnished with plenty of roots. It is difficult to have, proportionally, too much root, but very easy to have too little. A large or tall shoot can be sustained under favourable nursery conditions by only rudimentary roots but under the stressful environment of the planting site top growth will be poor, even sickly until new roots develop. It is not uncommon for this problem of imbalance to be exacerbated by over-zealous root pruning at lifting and at planting.

Plants should show reasonable recent shoot extension as indicated by spacing of buds. Tightly packed buds on the leading shoot are a sign of poor or checked growth in the nursery.

For larger trees, branch and crown form should be considered. Frequently the leading shoot is cut out to encourage a bushy crown (branched head), but this shape may conflict with objectives in many instances where tall specimen trees are desired.

38295

PLATE 30
Spindly, unbalanced trees have little prospect for successful growth.

Root collar diameter

Although height is used most commonly to grade plants into different categories, the best criterion for quality is thickness of the root collar. Sturdy plants with a thick root collar are more likely to regenerate new roots after planting. For a 30 cm tall plant a root collar diameter of *at least* 5 mm is desirable. For larger size plants see Table 7.1.

Ordering and receipt of plants

Timing

Plants should be ordered during the summer before planting is intended and delivery requested as close as possible to time of intended planting. With bare-rooted material, nurserymen will generally begin lifting in November. At the time of ordering it is useful to visit the nursery itself to inspect the beds and to request a sample of plants being raised in order to determine quality.

Quantity

It is prudent to order 10% above requirement to allow for on-site culling and other wastage.

Sources

There are a few 'forest' nurseries producing a narrow range of tree species, but, in general, the cost per plant from them will be low owing to economies of scale. Many nurseries supply a wide range of ornamental species of varying sizes. A list of such nurseries is found in the Horticultural Trades Association handbook and horticultural magazines. Most nurseries also advertise in the local telephone directory.

Receipt of plants

Plants should be delivered in good condition. As well as checking numbers and species, check all bags or trays of plants looking for signs of damage (breakages), fungal growth, insect pests and signs of drying-out. Any suspect plant can be further examined by nicking the bark (thumbnail): if green or greenish white it is still alive; if creamy white, brownish or brown it is dead or dying. If significant numbers of plants (more than 5%) appear in poor condition, the purchaser should consider rejecting the whole consignment.

Handling plants

Young trees are tender plants which easily suffer damage. A damaged or dying tree is a waste, even more so if it gets planted. Two requirements must be satisfied if plants are to be kept healthy:

1. roots must be kept moist;
2. plants should be treated very gently and handled with care.

Desiccation

Any exposure of roots to drying quickly kills the finer ones and, in a few hours, the main ones as well. Plants should be kept in the shade at all times to avoid overheating in bags and to keep the roots in moist condition. When transporting plants on open lorries their roots should be in polythene bags and the whole load covered with a well-secured tarpaulin.

Physical damage

All casual handling does harm and will reduce survival after planting. It is therefore essential not to drop plants, pile bags one on top of the other, or throw them about.

8 Establishment and early maintenance

Introduction

Having secured good quality plants which have been well wrapped and carefully handled and transported to the planting site, the next problem is how to establish them successfully. This is a stage in the life of an urban tree when it receives most attention, but unfortunately this attention is frequently misguided and even wasteful. There is a tendency to concentrate resources at planting when it would be better to spread these throughout the crucial early years of establishment. It should also be remembered that however much money is spent on planting, if a tree is of poor quality or has been mishandled or if site preparation is inadequate, it will not thrive.

Planting techniques

The choice of planting technique will depend on the size of plant used and on the site.

Notch planting

Bare-rooted transplants can be notch planted, a technique common in forest plantings. Slits are cut in the soil and held open with a spade while the tree's roots are carefully inserted so that they spread downwards (see Figure 8.1). Several types of notch can be used; a straight slit, an 'L' or a 'T' shape. The notch must be well-firmed around the tree, while pulling the plant gently upwards, so that the original root collar is at ground level. On clay soils the notch can open in dry weather and this technique is not suitable here.

If the ground is not bare, the notch can be cut into the sward and weed control applied later. Alternatively, a square of turf can be cut out first and either removed with the notch being cut directly into the exposed soil ('screef planting'), or inverted with the notch being cut through the turf ('turf planting'). Both these

1. Make plenty of room for the transplants roots

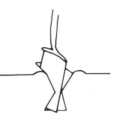

2. Ensure that the roots are pushed down as far as possible

3. Withdraw the transplant slightly to spread roots

4. Firm up to exclude air pockets

5. Transplant in correct position

FIGURE 8.1
The notch planting technique.

methods give a measure of weed control, but are not usually sufficient. Turf planting has the advantage of providing a better-drained planting position.

Pit planting

Larger planting stock and containerised plants should be pit planted. The size of pit will depend on the extent of the root system, but the pit must accommodate the root ball without the outer roots becoming bent and with the original root collar at final ground level once the soil has been firmed. Container stock should always be removed from the container, as even biodegradable containers can inhibit lateral root development. Plants which have badly coiled roots should be rejected. The roots which were against the edge of the container should be gently loosened to encourage lateral spread. The tree should be gently shaken during the process of filling the pit to ensure good contact between the roots and the soil.

If the tree is to be staked (see pp. 81–82), the stake should be inserted into the pit before the tree is planted to avoid damage to the roots. It should be placed on the windward side of the tree.

It is essential to ensure that water is freely draining from the pit or anaerobic conditions will result. Problems of this nature are usually caused by inadequate site preparation.

The planting medium

Unless the topsoil has been removed from the planting site or it is of unsuitable material (see Chapter 5), it is usually sufficient to backfill the planting pit with the soil that has been removed. This avoids any problems of interface between different materials at the edges of the pit.

Soil ameliorants

Compaction and poor soil structure are common problems on urban tree planting sites, resulting in impeded water movement and poor aeration. These are problems which should be addressed before planting (see Chapter 5). Soil ameliorants are not usually necessary and at best improve only the soil within the pit, causing potential problems when the roots reach the edge of the pit. There is a wide variety of so-called soil ameliorants available today, from traditional peat or manure to polyacrimide gels and seaweed derivatives.

1. ORGANIC MATTER

The addition of peat or other bulky organic matter to the planting pit backfill is a common practice. It can improve the structure and water-retaining ability of freely draining sandy soils, but experimental evidence shows little or no benefit in tree survival and growth even on sites known to have poor physical properties. The use of peat or other bulky organic materials can lead to problems:

a. enhanced water retention can exacerbate anaerobic conditions in clay soils;

b. interfaces between the backfill and the surrounding soil can open up in dry weather and expose roots;

c. if the inflow of air into the soil is restricted, as is often the case in urban sites, oxidation of the organic matter can reduce soil oxygen available to tree roots;

d. soil in the planting pit can become nitrogen-deficient as micro-organisms acting on peat absorb nitrogen;

e. contamination of the soil by the fungus *Phytophthora* can occur when farmyard manure is used;

f. the high pH of mushroom compost can damage young trees.

Non-bulky organic materials such as bone meal and dried blood are not subject to the problems listed above and can act as a slow-release supply of nutrients.

2. INORGANIC FERTILISERS

Some urban soils are deficient in nutrients essential for tree growth, but in general there is little need to add artificial fertilisers and indiscriminate use can be detrimental to the tree and the environment.

During its first growing season, the fine roots of bare-rooted stock are regenerating after losses during transplanting. The larger roots that survive planting are unable to take up large quantities of nutrients. Inorganic nitrogen added to the backfill at planting is likely to have leached from the pit before fine roots have regenerated and are able to take it up.

It is essential to ensure that weeds are cleared from around the base of the tree as they compete for nitrogen already in the soil and benefit from added fertilisers, becoming more vigorous and thereby increasing moisture stress.

On weed-free sites the use of a fertiliser at planting may promote shoot growth, but this can lead to an even greater imbalance in root:shoot ratio than that already caused by transplanting. It can also lead to root scorch. The addition of phosphorus-rich fertilisers to the backfill may be worthwhile as phosphorus is not readily leached from the soil and can induce greater root growth. See p. 90 for addition of fertilisers after planting.

3. WATER-RETAINING GELS

Polyacrimide water-retaining gels which can absorb up to 300 times their dry weight of water are used in horticulture to increase the water-retaining capacity of the soil and hence reduce irrigation costs. These products are already used in arboriculture although their effect on the survival and growth of young trees has not yet been fully tested.

They may be of value in providing a store of water to help the tree through periods of drought, but their use should be viewed as an additional expense which is unnecessary if water is not a limiting factor. If they are used, care should be taken to follow manufacturers' instructions as large amounts can cause the soil to swell excessively and alter the position of the tree in the planting pit.

4. OTHER AMELIORANTS

There are a range of other products, several of them derivatives of seaweed. These can act as a rich supply of nutrients, but the same cautions apply as for other organic fertilisers (see p. 79). Seaweed products can contain levels of boron which may be harmful to trees.

As with all other ameliorants, their use should be carefully considered. It may be that the resources spent on them would be better allocated to obtaining higher quality plants, more intense site cultivation to improve soil physical properties or to after-care.

Conditions at planting

Time of planting (i.e. autumn or spring) will have been decided before the plants are ordered (see Chapter 7). During the planting season, however, there can be a considerable variation in climatic conditions. It is important to choose a planting date

to minimise adverse effect on the newly-planted trees. Planting should be avoided when the soil is frozen.

Watering

On most urban tree planting sites in Britain, the amount of soil moisture is unlikely to be a limiting factor in tree growth, although it may not be readily available to the tree. Artificial irrigation of the tree pit is an expensive operation and should only be necessary under extreme conditions such as drought. If it is undertaken, it is important to ensure that the water is applied to maximum effect. Irrigation should aim to keep the whole root system moist by applying sufficient quantities of water at regular intervals and not by saturating at one point intermittently. Systems which apply the water below ground level avoid the problems of surface runoff.

It cannot be too strongly emphasised that weeds around the base of newly-planted trees can create soil moisture deficits. Good weed control reduces and often eliminates the need for irrigation. The use of mulch mats has the dual advantages of suppressing weeds and preventing evaporation from the soil surface.

Pruning of roots and shoots at planting

If planting stock is of high quality, with a good balance between roots and shoots, there should be no need to carry out pruning before planting except to remove any damaged material. It is widely believed, however, that the removal of a proportion of the shoots, thereby reducing the transpirational area during the early part of the growing season, will benefit the tree. This has not been proved in experimental work on pruning, where removal of none, half or all the branches of rowan standards at planting made no difference to early survival or growth. It is important that this technique is not seen as a panacea for poor quality plants.

'Stumping back' of plants by cutting the stem off near to ground level is a more extreme version of the above. It can have advantages where the tree is badly damaged or poorly-formed in that a new straight stem can be produced (although many trees will produce several coppice shoots) and the new growth is generally more vigorous.

D. Patch

FIGURE 8.2
Effect of staking on height and diameter increment of rowan standards.

Staking

The primary purpose of staking is to support large planting stock (i.e. standards) after planting while the root system regenerates to form a new anchorage. The imbalance in root:shoot ratio caused by transplanting is gradually redressed and the tree should become stable. The time taken for this process depends on the extent of the root system at planting and on the general health of the tree, but should not be more than 1–2 growing seasons. Failure of the trees to become self-supporting after this time may indicate inadequate root development caused by poor soil conditions.

The practice of using tall stakes, supporting the tree high into the crown, is commonly believed to reduce physical damage to the tree from strong winds or vandalism. Experimental evidence, however, contradicts this theory. Trees that are supported high up the stem put on less diameter growth below the tie and more height growth than trees with a short stake or none at all (see Figure 8.2). This creates a more unstable tree which relies on the stake for support. It is more prone to damage, especially at the point where the tie is fastened. Any force applied to a tree with a short or no stake can be dissipated over a greater length of stem. The problem of trees developing permanently bent upper stems in very windy areas is also

PLATE 31
The use of a short stake and a large weed-free area is sound practice for successful tree establishment.

PLATE 32
Successful staking of large standards (however, the supports should not be retained beyond two seasons). Note also the successful weed and grass control.

avoided. The use of smaller planting stock should be considered under these conditions.

Once in place, stakes and ties must be properly maintained. Two serious problems resulting from lack of maintenance are stem abrasion and strangulation. If a tree is incorrectly tied to a stake, movement of the tree causes the stem to rub against the stake, causing a wound which can be invaded by pathogens and weakens the tree leaving it susceptible to breakage. If ties are not adjusted as the tree grows, they will eventually tighten around the stem. This can cause changes in the cell structure of the stem at that point, weakening it. Ultimately the tie will strangle the tree, killing the crown above it.

Multiple staking is a technique for supporting large containerised stock where a single stake cannot be driven into the ground close to the stem. Two or more stakes are placed at the edge of the root ball and the tree is held upright between them by ties.

Good staking practice

Recommended practice for staking is as follows.

Avoid trees that need staking wherever possible. Smaller planting stock are generally easier to establish (see Chapter 7).

If the use of standards is unavoidable, choose healthy trees with a good root system that is capable of regenerating quickly and providing anchorage.

Use a stake no higher than one-third of the height of the tree.

Secure the tree to the stake using a single tie at the top of the stake. Rubber or plastic ties are best – those reinforced with metal or synthetic webbing must be inspected and adjusted at least twice a year. Some ties are self-adjusting and will eventually fall off, but they should be inspected occasionally.

Remove the stake as soon as the tree is self-supporting. This is usually at the start of the second growing season, which allows the root system time to develop before the onset of winter gales.

Trees that have been staked for many years will be dependent on the support, which must then be gradually reduced. The height of stake can be reduced and the tree secured by only one tie. If, after removal of the tie, the tree remains upright, it is probably safe to remove the support completely.

PLATE 33
Poor practice leads to unsightly results.

PLATE 34
This tree would have benefited from a large
(1 metre diameter) grass-free area at its base.

PLATE 35
City centre planting, Newcastle-upon-Tyne.

Protection

Urban trees suffer damage from many different agents ranging from deer in woodland-type environments to voles on motorway verges, and people, vehicles and machinery in built-up areas. Rabbits are rarely absent from planting sites and cattle, sheep, horses and goats in adjacent fields can lean over a fence and nibble foliage.

Protection of trees can be done either collectively using a physical barrier or, more commonly, on an individual tree basis. There are several types of individual guards, the choice depending on the likely predators. Table 8.1 gives specifications of guards for different problems.

Vole guards

Voles are periodically a problem on roadside plantings, especially where long grass is allowed to develop. Vole runs can be seen under the vegetation and the voles strip the bark off the lower stem and branches and can kill or seriously damage quite large plants. Well-weeded trees suffer less, as voles are reluctant to cross bare ground, but are not immune if populations are high.

If voles are the only problem (i.e. if the area is at least rabbit-proof), then small plastic vole guards can be used. These consist of split plastic tubes which coil around the tree, expanding as the tree grows and finally falling off. They are too small in diameter for voles to nest inside, but should be pushed into the ground for at least 5 mm to prevent access. A height of 200 mm is usually sufficient, but on rough ground or where there are tall weeds a height of 250–300 mm should be used.

Spiral rabbit guards

These are loosely coiled plastic tubes, usually with ventilation holes. They can reduce bark stripping by rabbits on the lower stem, but are only suitable for use on trees with sufficient side branches to hold them up (feathered whips or light standards) with a stem diameter of at least 25 mm.

Plastic mesh guards

These are rigid, photo-degradable polyethylene netting tubes of various diameters and heights used to protect trees against rabbits, deer and livestock. They are not effective against voles, but are fairly resistant to vandalism. Rabbits can chew through the plastic, but this only occurs when populations are high.

The guards are supplied in two types.

1. Mesh size 15 mm × 15 mm, ready cut to make a guard 75 mm diameter × 1.2 m height for protection against roe deer browsing (but not fraying). Can be cut in half to make 0.6 m height for protection against rabbits only. They are not suitable for use with small transplants, or those with pendulous leading shoots as these tend to grow through the mesh. Stems must be at least 25 mm away from the mesh to prevent rabbit damage.

2. Mesh size 25 mm × 35 mm, supplied on rolls 0.45 m or 1.0 m wide. Can be cut to make a tube of diameter 150 mm or 300 mm (for larger trees and shrubs) and any height.

Plastic mesh guards can be used on any size of tree to protect the main stem and leading shoot (but see 1 above). They are designed to degrade within 5–10 years, but should be checked

Table 8.1 Protection methods

| | Agent of damage | | | | | |
	Vole	Rabbit	Hare	Roe deer	Other deer	Stock
Vole guard	√	X	X	X	X	X
Spiral guard	√	√	X	X	X	X
Plastic mesh guard:						
0.6 m	X	√	X	X	X	X
1.2 m	X	√	√	√	X	X
1.8 m						
Treeshelter:						
0.6 m	X	√	X	X	X	X
1.2 m	X	√	√	√	X	X
1.5–1.8 m	X	√	√	√	√	√

Note: Specifications for height of guard must be increased on steeply sloping ground or where high snowfall is likely.

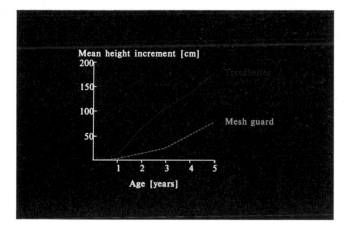

FIGURE 8.3
Comparison of early height growth for trees protected by mesh guard or treeshelter.

occasionally to ensure that fast-growing trees are not strangled and that leading shoots are free.

The netting is wrapped around the tree and the edges fastened with metal rings. It is important that the tree is central in the guard. With small trees the guard should be fastened to a firm support, usually a wooden stake which should not exceed the height of the guard or stem abrasion can result. Larger trees will support the guard by their stem and branches. Basal wire anchor pins can be used, but are only successful in firm soil types.

Stronger mesh guards, 35 mm × 35 mm, are available for protection against cattle, but adequate support for the guards is essential.

Height growth in plastic mesh guards is slightly better than in unprotected trees because the stem is supported (see Figure 8.3), but as for staking, diameter growth is proportionally reduced. This effect is minimal with short guards (0.6 m).

Treeshelters

Treeshelters are translucent polypropylene tubes, usually 1.2 m tall, which protect trees from a wide range of predators and provide a favourable microclimate around the tree by acting as a mini-greenhouse. Most tree species grow faster in height in treeshelters, with small transplants often reaching the top of the shelter by the second growing season (see Figure 8.3). Once the tree emerges from the shelter, stem diameter growth increases in response to greater stem movement. After about 5 years, the tree will have reverted to a normal height:diameter ratio, although in effect it will have gained several years' growth over unsheltered trees.

Most trees grow well in treeshelters although the natural form of conifers does not lend itself to the 1.2 m shelter. Half-size (0.6 m) shelters have been used successfully to protect conifers against rabbit damage where the cost of fencing was prohibitive.

Treeshelters have not been widely used in truly urban situations, probably because they are not suitable for whips and standards which are commonly planted. Transplants, however, generally establish better anyway (see Chapter 7) and with the added benefit of a treeshelter can catch up with and overtake larger planting stock very quickly.

Another worry about treeshelters in urban areas is that of vandalism. It is thought that they are more likely to invite trouble than more traditional guards and may even be stolen. This problem may diminish as treeshelters become more wide-spread, and the advantages of being able to establish healthy, vigorous trees much more quickly and at a lower cost may well warrant more trials in some urban situations.

Treeshelters give a measure of protection against voles and should be pushed well into the soil if damage is likely. Voles can burrow under treeshelters, especially on exposed sites where shelters may lift slightly off the ground. If the problem is serious, vole guards can be used inside. Treeshelters are supported by means of a stake, at least 25 mm × 25 mm, which must be driven well into the ground and be slightly shorter than the shelter to avoid stem abrasion.

Treeshelters are photodegradable and need not be removed. Due to the accelerated early height growth, trees in shelters need support for their first 5 years while they redress the balance between height and stem diameter. Modern treeshelters are designed to last at least this long. Larger pieces of the shelter material should be collected and removed when degrade occurs, to prevent litter problems. Some shelters have removable ties, making inspection or replacement of trees easier. Recent designs of shelter incorporate a softened or reflexed top edge to avoid damage to the stem and it is important to ensure that these are used the right way up.

Treeshelters are a very useful tool in successful establishment, but they are by no means a substitute for good quality plants or adequate maintenance. They do make trees easier to find and application of herbicide to control weeds can be done with little risk of damage.

Other methods of protection

There are many other methods of individual tree protection, from simple metal cages to elaborate structures more common in a parkland situation. When a high degree of protection against animals or humans is necessary, it is more cost-effective to protect groups of trees especially if survival is likely to be low.

Protection from damage to roots is also essential, especially where trees are planted in areas where soil compaction is likely to be severe such as shopping precincts or car parks. Guards can either prevent access to the area immediately around the tree or can cover the soil with a metal grid.

Careful design can provide protection for the tree without being visually obtrusive and may even serve other purposes.

Weed control

Weeds compete with trees for moisture, light and space. On urban sites where a mown grass sward is often present or established at the time of planting, competition for water and nitrogen can be very severe.

Young trees planted into a grass sward often show classic stress symptoms: sparse small leaves, shoot dieback and a yellowing of foliage due to nitrogen deficiency. Stressed trees often lose their leaves earlier at the end of the season. Table 8.2 shows the results of foliar sampling from a weed control experiment.

Results from experiments show that tree growth is reduced in the presence of weeds (see Figure 8.4). It should be noted that growth was worst in mown grass plots where regular cutting has invigorated the sward, thereby increasing soil moisture deficits.

Where there is some other stress-inducing factor affecting trees, weed control can have a dramatic effect on survival. Figure 8.5 shows the survival of poor quality oak transplants with and without weed control.

Table 8.2 The effect of three weeding regimes on first season's growth and foliar nutrient concentrations of wild cherry transplants

	Mown sward	Unmown sward	Bare soil
Height growth (cm)	9	31	80
Diameter growth (cm)	3	7	14
Foliar nutrient concentrations (% dry weight)			
N	2.6	2.5	3.4
P	0.19	0.17	0.20
K	1.06	1.05	1.64

Methods of weed control

There are several methods of controlling weeds around newly-planted trees, but to be effective it is essential that the weeds are killed or removed entirely, including the roots. Cutting is not effective and does no more than prevent small trees being smothered by tall weeds.

CULTIVATION

Pre-planting cultivation provides a weed-free planting site, but weeds often re-invade and require subsequent control. Removal of weeds by hoeing around the tree is effective if care is taken not to damage shallow roots, but this is very labour-intensive.

HERBICIDE

The use of herbicide is an effective and economical method of weed control. There is a range of approved herbicides for forestry use, some of which can be applied in the winter and have residual action (see Forestry Commission Field Book 8). Whichever one is used, the risk of damage to the tree must be minimised by careful application. Results from experiments show that growth is only slightly reduced if a small clump (about 10 cm diameter) of weeds is left around the base of the tree to avoid accidental spray damage to the stem.

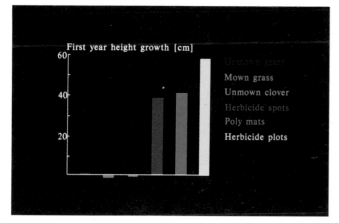

First year height growth [cm]

Unmown grass
Mown grass
Unmown clover
Herbicide spots
Poly mats
Herbicide plots

FIGURE 8.4
Effect of weeding on first year height growth of silver maple.

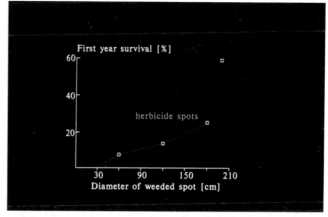

First year survival [%]

herbicide spots

Diameter of weeded spot [cm]

FIGURE 8.3
Survival of poor quality oak in relation to area of spot weeding around transplant.

MULCHING

There are several different materials that can be used to control weeds by smothering them or by preventing their growth. To be effective the mulch must prevent light reaching the soil and must remain impenetrable for 2–3 years. Organic mulches, such as bark or wood chips, are often colonised by weeds much more quickly than this and become ineffective.

Sheet mulches are generally more effective, but must be of a durable material. Those based on paper products or woven materials can disintegrate or allow weeds to grow through them. Black polythene of at least 500 gauge with ultra-violet inhibitor was the most effective of a range of those tested in mulching trials. It can be bought on the roll or as pre-prepared mats.

Mulch mats must be well secured by digging in the corners, and, on exposed sites or where vole damage is expected, should be weighted down with stones or clods of earth.

GROWTH RETARDANTS

The use of chemicals to retard the growth of grass swards is common in the management of sports turfs. If the transpiration of the sward can be significantly reduced, then the detrimental effect on tree growth is likely to be less, but early results from experiments suggest that this effect is likely to be small, with trees in bare ground doing much better.

ALTERNATIVE GROUND COVER

Broadleaved weeds are generally less competitive than grass and may vary in their effect on tree growth. They also tend to start growing later in the growing season, allowing the tree to get a head start. Leguminous plants can enhance nitrogen levels and may be useful on deficient soils. The use of shrubs around the tree base can prevent the development of a grass sward, deter vandalism and add to the æsthetic value of the planting. However, any vegetation immediately around the tree base will compete to some degree for water and nutrients. During early establishment years this is likely to reduce survival and growth.

Area of weeding

Experiments have shown that the minimum area required to be kept free from weeds around a newly-planted tree is a 1 m diameter spot. This area should be increased to at least 1.5 m diameter for large planting stock (whips and standards).

Plates 36–39 show 3-year-old sycamore transplants grown on a sandy site in Hampshire with different areas of weed control. Although the tree in the 0.6 m × 0.6 m herbicide square is healthier than that in the untreated area with no weed control, it is much smaller than that in the 1.2 m × 1.2 m herbicide square.

PLATES 36–39
Sycamore photographed in July 1985, 16 months after planting as 42 cm transplants on an infertile sand.

Upper left – no weed control;

Upper right – a 1.2 × 1.2 m area kept weed-free with herbicides;

Lower left – a 1.2 × 1.2 m black polythene mulch;

Lower right – a very large, 10 × 8 m, black polythene mulch.

On impoverished sites such as this even sparse weed growth is highly detrimental.

Its foliage is also yellower, indicating moisture and/or nitrogen stress due to the effect of weeds growing too close to it.

Timing of weeding

For maximum survival and growth, newly-planted trees should be free from weed competition from the start of their first growing season. Ideally, weed control should start before the trees are planted as newly-planted trees are most sensitive to competition during the early part of the growing season when root growth is vital. In a normal season a grass sward becomes active from March/April and should be controlled by this time.

In an experiment investigating the effect of the timing of weed control, black polythene mulch mats were laid down around newly-planted trees on different dates during the first growing season. The effect on tree growth can be seen in Figure 8.6. Although weed control as late as September appears to give some small advantage over unweeded trees or those with autumn weeding only, there is a marked reduction in growth with later application of mats.

With the use of herbicides, possible damage to the trees must be considered when deciding when to apply a herbicide. Mid-season applications run the risk of accidental damage to the tree as well as allowing competition to develop before control is applied. Winter applications of a residual herbicide avoid the risk and can give good control of grass during the important early part of the season.

Weed control is essential in the first year after planting and will result in improved growth for the first 3–4 years, depending on the relative growth of weeds and trees. Once the trees are well-established, weed control is no longer necessary, but if the trees are in an area of mown grass, maintenance of a weed-free area around the base will continue to reduce the likelihood of damage to the stem from mowing machinery.

Intensity of weeding

Ideally, the area immediately around the base of the tree should be kept completely free from weeds throughout the growing season. In many situations this is not practicable and the marginal benefit from killing the last few weeds is not justified.

Figure 8.7 shows the effect on young sycamore transplants of different intensities of weed control: from 1 to 14 applications of glyphosate in the first growing season. The growth response of the trees is directly proportional to the intensity of weeding. Highly intensive application of herbicide is neither economical nor environmentally desirable; but this degree of weed control is attainable with the use of effective mulches.

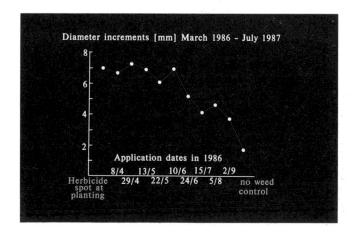

FIGURE 8.6
Effect of different application dates of mulch mats on diameter increment of wild cherry.

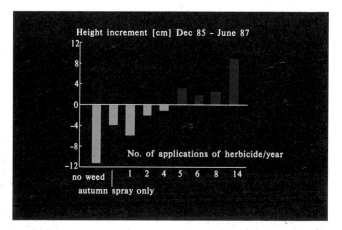

FIGURE 8.7
Effect of different intensities of herbicide weeding on height increment of sycamore.

Fertilising

See p. 79 for addition of fertilisers at planting.

If, despite good weed control, trees show signs of nutrient deficiency during early establishment, the addition of fertilisers may be necessary. It is advisable to carry out foliar analysis to determine which, if any, nutrients are lacking because similar symptoms can result from poor physical conditions in the soil. Foliar analysis should not be carried out until the second growing season, by which time the tree should have reached equilibrium with the site, and any nursery deficiencies overcome.

Deficiency symptoms

(On fully developed leaves in full light)

NITROGEN – yellowing of the whole crown, reduced leaf size, leaves uniformly discoloured.

PHOSPHORUS – stunted, dull-green leaves. Purple or red tints at leaf margin in severe cases.

POTASSIUM – yellowing of leaves, sometimes between veins, with marginal scorch in severe cases. Leaves inside crown may be less affected.

MAGNESIUM – slight yellowing of leaves, especially between the veins where dead patches may develop in severe cases.

Other deficiencies are rare, except on specialised soil types, e.g. lime-induced chlorosis on soils with a very high pH.

Foliar sampling

Leaves may be analysed to indicate nutrient deficiencies. Fully-expanded, undamaged foliage from the outside of the crown, exposed to full light, should be taken from late July to early August for broadleaves and larch, and from early October to mid-November for conifers.

For broadleaves, enough leaves should be taken to cover an A4 sheet; for conifers, five current year's shoots from the whorl below the leader. Samples from several trees should be amalgamated if necessary. Samples must be clearly labelled and packed in polythene bags for immediate despatch to a laboratory for analysis.

Application of fertilisers

If fertilisers are required, they can be applied in late March either as a top dressing or in dibber holes. It is essential to ensure that weed control is rigorous or the benefits from fertilising will be outweighed by enhanced competition from the invigorated sward.

SECTION 4

Aftercare and Management

The care of established trees is often neglected, with the result that investment in early work is lost and serious management problems arise. This section provides advice on aftercare. It should be noted that Chapters 10 and 11 are technical in character and aimed principally at providing guidance for consultants, contractors and other professionals engaged in tree operations.

9 Managing the growing trees

In the years after planting, attention must be given to a variety of factors that can threaten the success of the initial investment in tree planting. Three main problem areas can be identified:
  unwanted weeds,
  tree protection,
  pruning practice.

Weeds

While herbaceous weeds threaten the initial establishment of trees (see Chapter 8) it is woody growth and climbing plants that give rise to problems later on and can cause serious damage even to the most vigorous of young trees.

Honeysuckle (*Lonicera periclymenum*) grows on a range of soils and can tolerate a moderate amount of shade, but in order to flower it must grow in full light. Young vigorous shoots grow from the base of the weed and snake around the stems of young trees. Honeysuckle stems have great strength and resist the annual girth increase of the tree's stem which becomes constricted, producing a spiral distortion, although in time it may overgrow the honeysuckle. This weakness may lead to stem snap by wind or by an accumulation of snow. Once honeysuckle is climbing a tree it is necessary to unwind the stems from the tree and then cut them at ground level. The root system may be pulled up or, once regrowth has commenced, poisoned with an appropriate herbicide (see Forestry Commission Field Book 8). Honeysuckle can grow to 6 metres above the ground and is capable of threatening young trees for many years until their foliage and branches shade out the weed. Once trees are out of danger, honeysuckle need not be removed. The low mounds it forms under closed canopies of woodlands can be a valuable ecological niche.

On chalky and high pH soils old man's beard (*Clematis vitalba*) can be a serious threat to young and maturing trees. Shoots sprout from the root-stock and sprawl over any low-growing plant; but they will climb 10 metres up trees, ranging from branch to branch. The petioles of the weed twist three or four times around a twig or stem of suitable diameter (1 cm). Large plants of old man's beard can lie on and blanket trees and shrubs which then become distorted, smothered or even broken. While the weed is blanketing trees and shrubs it cannot be treated safely with a herbicide. Manual and mechanical pulling of the *Clematis* needs to be done along with cutting (secateurs are best) or pulling up the roots. Re-growth and seedling plants can be treated with an appropriate herbicide (see Forestry Commission Field Book 8) if done early in the year and provided the planted trees are protected from the chemical.

Ivy (*Hedera helix*) and other climbing plants are usually less troublesome to trees. If they are extremely vigorous and threaten to swamp a tree they should be removed.

While these climbers are generally woodland weeds, they can also be a localised problem in roadside and parkland plantings. All plantings should be checked periodically for these weeds so that appropriate early remedial action can be taken.

Once trees are established a common aim is to maintain a formal appearance by more or less intensive grass cutting. In these positions, clusters of herbaceous weeds can develop around the base of young trees and although less damaging to the established tree, they may look unsightly. Filament cutters (e.g. strimmers) must never be allowed to contact the bark of the tree, as even thick bark of a maturing tree is cut through by the filament. This may leave the tree vulnerable to pathogens, or if the stem is girdled the tree may die or regrow as coppice.

Mechanical damage is often inflicted on the young trees as a result of grass cutting machines being driven carelessly or too close to the trees. If low branches make the weeds inaccessible the branches may be broken (or the machine operator injured). The need for machines to pass close to the base of trees can be reduced if herbicides are used to maintain bare earth or a mulch is placed around each tree. Strategically placed large stones or short stakes can be positioned around each tree as protection, but control of the weeds will still be needed.

Protection

Fencing, individual guards or treeshelters must be maintained in an effective condition. Replacement of stakes or guards is expensive and it will usually be cost effective to avoid such maintenance due to failure of components by selecting materials which have a life at least as long as the planned protection period. There will always be a need for routine inspections followed by remedial maintenance or recovery of materials.

Studies in the United States and Britain have shown that neglect of stakes and ties leads to severe damage to trees. Recommendations for staking can be found in Chapter 8.

Litter and fires

Throughout urban areas improvements to the environment are often frustrated by man's activities. Nowhere is this more obvious than with litter and fire.

Once litter has been dropped it blows around until it is collected, becomes marooned in a 'backwater' or lodged among trees and shrubs. Litter is unsightly rather than directly damaging to the plants. However, if allowed to remain it can form a readily combustible fuel stock which, if ignited, could destroy the whole planting. Even individual trees in a street can be vulnerable. Unfortunately, tree guards designed to protect trees can act as litter bins unless secured so that litter falls through and blows away.

Plantations, especially those on urban fringes, may attract unauthorised tipping of rubbish. If clearance is not undertaken promptly, the public's perception of the area will change for the worse and further rubbish will be added.

Pruning

The frequency of inspections and prescriptions for formative pruning must recognise not only the requirements of the design objectives throughout the life of the tree but also whether there is a question of risk to people and property. For example, pruning individual trees in a woodland is seldom justified as thinning can be employed to remove trees with undesirable characteristics during the development of the woodland. This option does not exist for street trees.

Some stem and crown defects in trees have their origin in the nursery. The majority of trees are bought by specification to British Standard 3936 *Specification for nursery stock*. This describes a number of forms and sizes of tree which do not relate to the natural growth of tree species. A birch for example will normally develop lateral branches along the stem, but to make an ash produce feathers the nurseryman must remove the apical dominance imposed by the terminal bud: he prunes the leading shoot. A number of previously suppressed lateral buds will then be stimulated into growth. This treatment may in time result in a broad crowned tree lacking the natural crown shape of the species, and within the crown there will be potentially weak forks which may split in high winds or after heavy snow.

The first requirement in formative pruning is to cut back to a point of active growth those shoots which following transplanting have died back and could serve as entry points for disease. Weak and unwanted shoots should be removed during this operation and potentially weak forks should be reduced by pruning to a single shoot. Wide sweeping lateral branches should be shortened to prevent them becoming competing leaders.

Another problem arising from poor plant material is the use, especially in towns, of ornamental cultivars propagated in the nursery by budding or grafting a scion on to a root stock. Unfortunately root stocks can be incompatible with the cultivar they support, and root stocks produce their own shoots from below the graft. If left unchecked (and in extreme cases pruning may be needed annually) these shoots can result in a 'scrub' developing, or the ornamental form may be swamped by the more vigorous species used as the root stock. The result is unsightly, and especially on streets it can be potentially hazardous. As a general rule it is true to say that trees growing on their own roots, although possibly more expensive to buy, are cheaper to maintain in the longer term.

In all aspects of tree management there is need for awareness of the implications of failing to provide necessary treatment at an early stage in the tree's life. A badly placed shoot or even a developing bud is easily and cheaply removed when young, but if left unchecked, not only is correction more difficult and expensive but the shape of the tree may be permanently damaged. Premature removal of the tree may then be the only recourse.

10 Pruning practice

It is important to understand that tree surgery nearly always creates injuries. This must be set against the common belief, in many respects justified, that such work is good for trees.

The first stage in minimising damage is to decide whether the work is really necessary. In many urban sites, trees may interfere with human activities or with buildings (see Chapter 12), and these considerations may dictate the arboricultural programme. If the need for severe surgery is unavoidable, it is essential to realise that it may greatly shorten the safe life of a tree by exposing it to invasion by decay fungi. This needs to be taken into account by those who consider planning applications. It would be preferable in some instances to admit that existing trees must be sacrificed and replaced by new plantings after development is complete, rather than to accept unrealistic plans for their retention.

Specific kinds of surgical work and their implications for disease and decay

Formative pruning

In many urban situations, such as parks and streets, trees may survive for many years provided that any changes to their surroundings are minor, compared with the traumas that can occur on development sites. There may nevertheless be some need to control their growth, especially if the species choice was not suitable for the site. It is essential that such work should be planned so that tree health and structural soundness are protected and perhaps enhanced. In this context it is particularly important that the development of the desired main branching structure should be achieved while trees are young. Formative pruning involves the removal of unwanted branches while they are small. It will often obviate the future need to remove major branches, thus avoiding the creation of large, decay-prone wounds.

By some definitions, 'pruning' is used only to describe the removal of twigs and small branches, and the term 'lopping' is

PLATE 40
Longitudinal section of stain in oak branch base.

sometimes understood to involve large branches. However, 'pruning' will be used in this text to include large and small branches alike.

Formative pruning is often based on tradition and on subjective concepts of desirable appearance, but the practice also provides the worthwhile opportunity of preventing the formation of weak forks. A weak fork is most likely to develop where the branching angle is very acute, a feature which occurs more in some species and cultivars than in others. Once they have begun to form, weak forks usually reveal their existence by the bifurcation of the ridge ('branch bark ridge') which marks the junction between the members of the fork.

Pollarding and topping

In this Handbook, pollarding is taken to mean the removal of a young tree's leading shoot in order to encourage several leaders to develop. The term topping is reserved here to describe the removal of the crown of a mature or semi-mature tree.

When a tree is pollarded, decay may develop beneath the cut, but it does not usually extend very far into wood which is laid down in later years. The new wood is protected by a natural barrier which is formed by the cambium in response to the injury. Since pollarding, as defined here, is carried out when the tree is young, there is potential for the development of a wide 'shell' of newly-formed, sound wood around this barrier as the tree grows. It is thus unusual for the main stem to become decayed to the extent of breakage, although basal breakage of individual leaders may occur due to the presence of decay near the point of pollarding. In towns, pollarding can make it possible to grow certain highly desired species which would otherwise become too tall for their surroundings. However, if re-pollarding is not carried out, the trees will usually attain their full height, albeit with a modified branching structure. Re-pollarding, once begun, should be repeated periodically, otherwise the leaders may break away from the pollarding point due to their increasing weight. This commitment may involve considerable expense, and a winter appearance which is often regarded as unsightly.

Topping and pollarding involve the severance of the main stem and thus expose its entire cross-section to possible decay. As explained above, the capacity for new wood formation in a young tree may counteract this problem. However, in the case of topping (which, by the above definition, involves the main stem

PLATE 41
A weak fork.

95

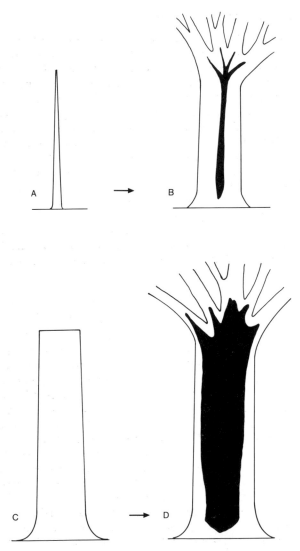

FIGURE 10.1
Consequences of pollarding and topping.
Left-hand side: at time of cutting.
Right-hand side: several years later.
Shaded zones, as seen in longitudinal section, indicate the likely maximum limits of staining and decay.
A→B Pollarding (as carried out on a young tree).
C→D Topping (as carried out on a mature or semi-mature tree).

of a mature or semi-mature tree), the old, vulnerable wood will occupy a large core in the middle of the tree even after the addition of many new annual rings (see Figure 10.1). Another problem is that the removal of most or all of a tree's crown, and hence of its photosynthetic capacity, is likely to impair its ability to defend itself against fungal attack. Topping is an inherently bad practice biologically, and should be considered only in exceptional circumstances.

Crown reduction and thinning

Urban trees are often subjected to a periodic crown reduction, rather than actual topping or re-pollarding. The purpose of this may be to keep large species in check, but it may have the more positive value of reducing the wind resistance of trees which are at a relatively high risk of windbreak or windthrow. In many cases, this reduction almost amounts to re-pollarding in the sense that branches are cut back fairly close to their points of origin. As with complete re-pollarding or topping, severe crown reduction imposes a commitment to repeat the operation periodically in order to limit the weight borne by partially decayed trunks or branch bases.

The term crown reduction means trimming the crown, involving the removal of relatively small branches and twigs. Crown thinning, while also involving twigs and minor branches, does not affect the height or spread of the crown. The small wounds produced in the course of thinning or moderate reduction are not likely to lead to the development of serious decay, but all cuts should be made at natural junctions so that dead snags will not be produced. It is also unwise to remove more than one-third of the crown volume for the reason mentioned in the section dealing with topping.

Cabling and bracing

Bracing rods or cables may be fixed to a tree in order to restrict the movement of forks or branches at any points of structural weakness. The insertion of rods or bolts involves wounding, but the wounds are small compared with major branch cuts and the benefits of the treatment generally outweigh the risk of decay developing. It offers the opportunity to retain structurally weak or decayed trees which may have considerable amenity value but which might otherwise have an unacceptably high 'hazard rating'. The suitability of a tree for cabling or bracing should be judged by a qualified arboricultural consultant since in some cases the overall condition of the tree renders such work an unwarranted expense, while in others it is not a safe alternative to more radical remedies such as crown reduction or felling. The correct techniques for inserting cable bolts are described in British Standard 3998, and should always be followed.

Factors influencing the development of disease and decay in association with arboricultural wounds

In any treatment which involves cutting stems or branches it is important to carry out the work so as to minimise the resultant risk of decay. Factors influencing this risk include the size of wounds, the species of tree and the time of year of wounding. The number of wounds on a single stem and the overall health of the tree are also thought to be important. Another major factor is the position of the cut in relation to the parent stem or branch, and this is explained in the section below on pruning practice.

Size of pruning wounds

The larger the wound, the greater the risk of decay. The reasons for this may be less obvious than they seem, and there is some evidence that the important factor is not so much the size of the wound, as the size of the severed branch relative to that of the main stem. There is no precise formula for calculating a safe size of wound, since many additional factors can influence the risk of decay developing. A rough guide, based on present knowledge, is that the *maximum* allowable diameter for a wound created on the main stem or on a major branch should be about one-quarter to one-third the diameter of the stem or branch itself. Exceptions can be made for the formative pruning of very young trees.

The size of a wound also affects the rate at which it is occluded by callusing. The larger the wound, the greater is the distance across which the callus must grow. This simple relationship is, however, influenced by the fact that, on any one stem, callus tends to grow faster on a large wound than on a small one.

Number of pruning wounds per tree

Decay associated with single wounds is very often confined to within a few centimetres of the wound surface, but it sometimes extends to the centre of the tree and may eventually develop into a central column. Such extended decay seems to occur more frequently where several or many wounds have been created on a single stem or branch, especially if they are large and perhaps even more so if they date from about the same time. The reason for this is probably that, like large wounds, multiple wounds severely disrupt the xylem function. It is not possible, in the current state of knowledge, to give guidance on the maximum allowable number of wounds on a given length of stem, but it is important to be aware of the risks inherent in multiple wounding and to avoid the practice wherever possible. There is some evidence that multiple injection wounds, as used on elm trees against Dutch elm disease, carry a similar risk, but this could be reduced by use of the newer and more efficient shallow injection techniques.

Position of pruning wounds in relation to the main stem

Pruning, like natural branch death, carries a risk of extended dieback and decay, perhaps more so because it is a sudden event. Severe cambial dieback following pruning is likely when a tree has been stressed by drought, transplanting or suppression. Extension of dieback and infection is usually limited by the formation of a natural barrier which tends to form at the base of the branch. The pruning position influences the effectiveness of this barrier. Flush pruning damages wood above the branch junction and thus exposes it to decay fungi. It also removes the tissue at the branch base in which the live/dead boundary would otherwise form. Boundaries are thus made to form deeper within the main stem and are more likely to fail. On the other hand, the retention of long stubs inhibits occlusion of the wound and may also encourage the development of decay. Some of these effects require further study but it seems advisable for the present to follow the guidelines for pruning position given below in the passages on pruning practice.

Susceptibility of different species to decay and cankering following pruning

Species, and indeed cultivars and individuals within species, differ in their ability to form effective barriers at pruning wounds, but too little research has yet been done for anyone to provide a 'league table' of susceptibility. To some extent, the differences are related not only to a general ability to lay down natural barriers, but also to resistance against certain disease-causing organisms. For example, many members of the Rosaceae are susceptible to infection by canker fungi, especially *Nectria* spp. Another common disease-causing organism which affects this family, as well as many others, is the silver leaf fungus, *Chondrostereum purpureum*, which can cause decay or be replaced by other decay fungi.

Many of those species which form a true heartwood are fairly resistant to decay, since most heartwoods contain substances which inhibit invasion by decay fungi. Heartwood is by no means immune from decay, and there are a number of fungi which are specialised heartwood rotters. A notable example is *Laetiporus sulphureus*, which attacks several genera and is common in oak, yew and false acacia.

Sapwood, unlike heartwood, is a living tissue which can lay down physical and chemical barriers, often very effectively, in response to injury or microbial attack. In heartwood-forming species, the chemicals formed in this reaction may be similar to those already present in the heartwood. In species which form no true heartwood, such as beech and most maples, the sapwood tends to become increasingly susceptible to fungal invasion and decay as it ages, since its resistance depends partly on the presence of living cells which gradually die over several decades.

The influence of time of year on pruning-induced cankering and decay

The time of year is significant mainly with respect to certain disease-causing organisms which require fresh wounds in order to infect the tree. There are, however, many decay fungi which seem to make their first appearance after a much longer period, perhaps many years. Nevertheless, it seems likely that seasonal variations in the ability of the tree to lay down strong barriers before such fungi arrive may influence the long-term outcome of wounding.

Research specifically concerned with silver leaf disease of rosaceous fruit trees caused by the fungus *Chondrostereum purpureum* has indicated that wounds made in June, July and August become infected much less often than those made in

other months. This is probably due to the varying seasonal resistance of the trees. No similar work has been done for other wood-invading fungi, but there is a certain amount of information available, also mainly concerning fruit trees, on canker fungi. Many of these tend to cause most damage when infection begins in the autumn, since they can attack the cambium over several months while the tree is dormant and has little ability to defend itself. Indeed, it seems that, in at least some species, cambial dieback may be at its worst in autumn prunings, even without the intervention of a particular fungal disease-causing organism.

Pruning practice

As mentioned above, pruning position may be an important factor in determining the effectiveness of the natural defences of a tree against the extension of dieback and decay. It was suggested that there is a correct pruning position, and this section describes in more detail the procedure for locating this position. It should first be emphasised that research is still needed in this area, since much of the evidence favouring the concept of a correct pruning position is based on observation rather than experiment.

Position of pruning wounds

Correct pruning is the creation of a wound which impinges neither on the xylem elements above the wound nor on the region of the branch junction where a natural barrier would be likely to form. There are two features of a branch junction which can help to locate this position. These are the branch bark ridge and the branch collar. The ridge is always present, unless it has been obscured by the formation of a very thick outer bark. It marks a plane of separation between branch and main stem (or parent branch) tissues, and it should never be injured in the course of cutting. The upper (distal) edge of the final cut should always begin just beyond the ridge (see Figure 10.2a). The cutting angle should, as shown in the figure, be a mirror image of the angle between the parent stem and the ridge. In accordance with standard practice, the final cut should only be made after most of the weight of the branch has been removed by two preliminary cuts (see Figure 10.2). More than two preliminary cuts may be needed for the safe removal of heavy or awkward branches.

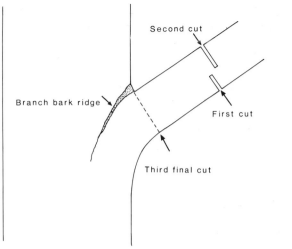

FIGURE 10.2a
Diagram of 'natural' pruning position on a branch junction with no 'collar'.

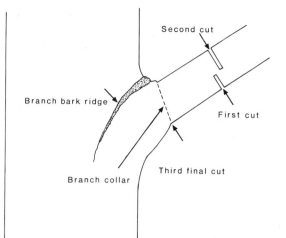

FIGURE 10.2b
Diagram of 'natural' pruning position on a branch junction with 'collar'.
(Note: this diagram applies equally to dead branch pruning.)

The advice concerning branch collars is rather more tentative. These seem to be formed when the diameter growth of the branch is very small in relation to that of the parent stem. Tree species vary in their tendency to produce collars. The best advice available at present is to make the cut immediately outside (i.e. distal to) the collar, irrespective of the position of the ridge (see Figure 10.2b). In many cases, the collar is present only on the underside (i.e. the proximal side) of the branch base. The top of the cut should then be just beyond the ridge and its bottom edge should be just beyond the collar.

Pruning tools

A smoothly cut wound is better than a rough one with regard to promotion of fungal growth and the risk of dieback, and for this reason a sharp bow-saw is a good practical choice for pruning. It is also light and easily carried while climbing in the crown. Some modern designs of pruning saw also provide a clean cut and are more easily inserted into tight crotches. They tend, however, to produce more friction than the very narrow blade of a bow-saw. Chainsaws may have to be used for removing large branches, but it should be remembered that large wounds should not be created without good reason. A sharp pruning knife should also

be carried to pare away any irregularities which may have been left around the edge of the wound.

It is not generally necessary to sterilise tools before use, but this should be done if they have been used on bark or wood which is infected with a canker fungus or an aggressive parasite such as the silver leaf fungus. Oily tools such as chainsaws cannot be properly sterilised and should not be used on highly infective material. A general disinfectant such as 'Dettol' or 'Jeyes' Fluid', diluted according to manufacturer's instructions, will suffice for most purposes, except where virus infection is a problem, but it is not possible for the user to know when the solution has lost its effectiveness. It is better to use a product based on sodium hypochlorite; either a laboratory grade, or a household bleach. The hypochlorite becomes exhausted during use, and it is important to make up a fresh solution every day. If possible, a product which also contains potassium permanganate ('Chloros') should be used, since decolorisation of the purple permanganate indicates that the hypochlorite has been exhausted. The concentrated solution should be diluted at the rate of one part to a hundred parts of clean water. The dilute solution must be made up freshly every day and stored in a clean, non-metallic container. Tools must be cleaned before sterilisation, since any dirt or grease will render the sterilant ineffective.

A few minutes' immersion will suffice for sterilisation. To prevent corrosion and possible damage to plant tissue, the sterilised tools should be rinsed in water or swabbed after immersion.

Use of wound dressings

There are four main approaches to the control of microbial infection in tree wounds.

1. The surface of the wound can be treated promptly with a durable sealant in the hope that infection will be excluded.

2. The wound tissues can be treated with a chemical fungicide or a biological control agent.

3. A treatment can be applied which makes the micro-environment of the wound tissues unsuitable for the growth of damaging fungi.

4. Callus growth across the surface of the wound can be encouraged in the expectation that decay development will cease once occlusion is complete.

A cosmetic covering to the wound may also be desired. A treatment applied in an attempt to follow any one of the above approaches may have several effects.

Most of the evidence on available commerical wound dressings suggests that physical exclusion of damaging fungi and maintenance of chemical activity against them can be obtained only for a short period (less than 1 year). Short-term protection may be very useful where the main risk is from a fresh wound parasite, such as *C. purpureum* or one of the more pathogenic canker fungi. It is not likely to help much against most decay fungi.

A somewhat longer term protection may be available from biological control agents, particularly species of the fungus *Trichoderma*. At least one product containing this fungus is commercially available for treating tree wounds.

The control of the wound micro-environment, particularly gaseous exchange, is also difficult to achieve in the long term, owing to the degradation of the dressing materials. Current work on novel wound treatments may, however, promise some advance in this approach.

Callus formation is enhanced for up to about 3 years by some sealants, but this is likely to be of little use on very small wounds which can be occluded rapidly anyway, or on very large wounds which may never become occluded. Experiments show that sealants containing the fungicide thiophanate methyl are particularly good at enhancing short-term callus growth. This fungicide has little activity against most decay fungi, although it inhibits attack by many canker fungi.

At the time of writing, new legislation on the use of pesticides and fungicides is being implemented in Britain. Until the full implications of this are known with regard to wound dressings, it is not appropriate to give specific recommendations for the use of the several categories of products. Definitive information will be provided in British Standard 3998 in due course.

11 Diseased and damaged trees

Trees harbour a wide range of fungi, bacteria, viruses, and animals such as insects and birds. These may affect their health and longevity, but rarely threaten the survival of forests and woodland. Indeed, they are seen as desirable in terms of wildlife conservation. In the urban setting, trees similarly provide important habitats for wildlife, but some of the animals and micro-organisms which they support may cause damage which is sufficient to result in a loss of amenity or even a hazard to safety. Urban conditions may also impose stress on trees, and this can contribute to damage. Some kinds of damage, especially those involving wood decay, may impose a need for preventive or remedial action. This chapter deals with damage which may occur in existing trees, rather than with problems relating to new planting. However, one of the options for managing damaged trees is their replacement and some guidance on this is given where appropriate.

Recognition of damage

The specific diagnosis of diseases, disorders and the identification of pest species is often a job for the specialist, but managers of urban trees need to be able to recognise the main types of problem that are likely to occur. There are a number of books and leaflets which can help the manager, and the most useful of these are shown in Further Reading (Appendix IV). The Forestry Commission leaflet *The recognition of hazardous trees* is particularly important with regard to public safety. Part of it is reproduced as Figure 11.1.

The type of damage must be identified before the management of damaged trees is considered. It may prove necessary to carry out remedial action, but there are many pests and diseases for which no treatment is appropriate. For some this is because no effective remedy exists, while for others the cost of treatment or the environmental hazards of chemical control may be major deterrents. Nevertheless, the diagnosis of a problem may help to avoid its recurrence. A guide to the main types of damage

likely to affect amenity trees is provided on pages 136–140 in the Further Information Section at the end of this Handbook (Appendix III).

Control of damage

There are a number of ways in which damage can be minimised thus prolonging the useful life of an urban tree and allowing it to attain the high amenity value which comes with maturity. The main strategies are as follows.

1. Avoidance of damage, which can be achieved wholly or partly in three main ways:
   a. control of damaging agents, which may for example involve the use of chemicals or the use of physical barriers;
   b. replacement of susceptible species with others which are more resistant to damage;
   c. improvement of growing conditions in order to make the trees more tolerant of or resistant to attack by pests and disease-causing organisms.
2. Treatment and management of damage already sustained.
3. Minimising damage caused by arboricultural practice, especially pruning (see Chapter 10).

These strategies are now considered in detail.

Avoidance of damage

One way of avoiding damage is to keep potentially damaging organisms away from trees, and this is feasible for certain mammals which can be excluded by tree guards or fencing (Chapter 8). A barrier on the tree itself, in the form of a grease band around the stem, can help to protect the crown from attack by certain invertebrate pests which do not fly, or which have non-flying stages which need to climb up or down stems in order to complete their life cycles.

In most urban situations, preventive treatment is often ruled

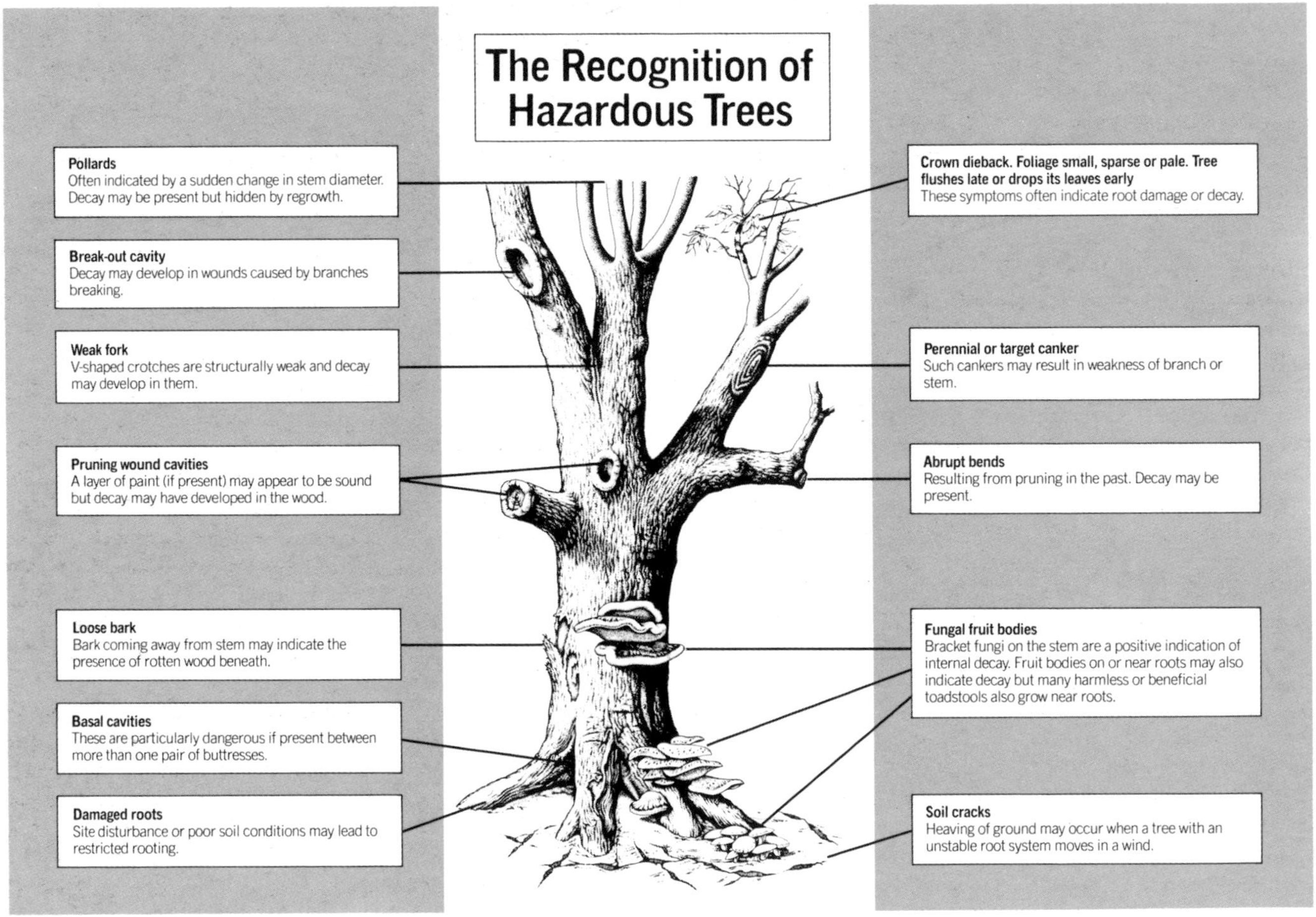

The Recognition of Hazardous Trees

Pollards
Often indicated by a sudden change in stem diameter. Decay may be present but hidden by regrowth.

Break-out cavity
Decay may develop in wounds caused by branches breaking.

Weak fork
V-shaped crotches are structurally weak and decay may develop in them.

Pruning wound cavities
A layer of paint (if present) may appear to be sound but decay may have developed in the wood.

Loose bark
Bark coming away from stem may indicate the presence of rotten wood beneath.

Basal cavities
These are particularly dangerous if present between more than one pair of buttresses.

Damaged roots
Site disturbance or poor soil conditions may lead to restricted rooting.

Crown dieback. Foliage small, sparse or pale. Tree flushes late or drops its leaves early
These symptoms often indicate root damage or decay.

Perennial or target canker
Such cankers may result in weakness of branch or stem.

Abrupt bends
Resulting from pruning in the past. Decay may be present.

Fungal fruit bodies
Bracket fungi on the stem are a positive indication of internal decay. Fruit bodies on or near roots may also indicate decay but many harmless or beneficial toadstools also grow near roots.

Soil cracks
Heaving of ground may occur when a tree with an unstable root system moves in a wind.

FIGURE 11.1
The recognition of hazardous trees.

out because it is environmentally undesirable or because the pest or disease problem is not very serious. Occasionally, a preventive treatment such as tar-oil winter wash can be used if a particularly valuable specimen tree is at serious risk from recurring attack by an insect pest or disease-causing organism. It is also conceivable that pest or disease problems in urban forestry projects may require solutions of a type more usually suited to commercial forestry. An example of pesticide use in forestry is the application of insecticides to transplants against attack by pests such as beetles in the genera *Hylobius* and *Hylastes*, which can kill young plants. This particular problem is mainly confined to areas where the pests build up to very high populations, for example where extensive tree-felling has taken place.

Remedial use of pesticides is often undesirable in urban areas, but certain products such as the bacterial control agent *Bacillus thuringiensis* can be used for the control of exceptionally troublesome pest species such as the browntail moth (*Euproctis chrysorrhoea*). The caterpillars of this insect can cause a human health problem by the release of their irritant hairs.

The other two avoidance strategies outlined at the beginning of this chapter were the replanting of sites with species or cultivars less liable to damage and the improvement of site conditions. Before adopting either of these strategies, it is necessary to be aware of the influence that site factors can have on the health of trees, not only directly but also through modifying their susceptibility to certain pest and disease problems. Thus some pests and diseases are confined to certain localities or regions because of their dependence on soil type, climate or pollution climate.

In Britain the best known example of a tree disease which is influenced by climate is sooty bark disease of sycamore (*Acer pseudoplatanus*) caused by the fungus *Cryptostroma corticale*. It causes serious damage or death only in certain years which follow summers in which the mean daily maximum temperature for June, July or August exceeds 23° C and it may be for this reason that it occurs mainly in the warmer parts of the UK. *Phytophthora* root rot is an example of a disease influenced by local conditions. This often lethal condition is favoured by poor drainage. The fungi which cause it have very wide host ranges but some tree species (e.g. Lawson cypress) are more susceptible than others (e.g. Leyland cypress), and it is worth bearing this in mind when replanting high-risk sites.

An insect problem which seems favoured by relatively warm conditions is the episodic build-up of browntail moth (*Euproctis chrysorrhoea*) populations. This pest seems to have a preference for the Rosaceae, but as it also attacks many other tree species, it may not be possible to solve the problem by replacement of existing trees.

Another factor believed to predispose trees to attack by certain pests and disease-causing organisms is air pollution, even where it is not causing obvious damage. On the other hand, districts where sulphur dioxide levels are high have a low incidence of certain foliar diseases such as black spot of roses (caused by *Diplocarpon rosae*) and tar-spot of sycamore (caused by *Rhytisma acerinum*).

Once a site-related problem has been recognised, possible solutions can be considered. In many cases replanting with a tolerant species or cultivar is the best option. For example frost-tolerant species can be used in a frost hollow. Where site amelioration is preferred, there is a further choice to be made, that is between replanting after amelioration (see Chapter 5) or attempting to improve the conditions while the existing trees remain *in situ*. Although the latter choice may often seem the most desirable, it is generally the less likely to succeed, particularly if the trees are affected not only by the unfavourable conditions, but also by associated root disease which may be irreversible.

Some improvement of conditions on difficult sites may be feasible if it does not involve further injury to the trees. For example, there are a number of machines on the market which can relieve the effects of compaction by injecting high pressure air into the soil at a depth of as much as a metre (e.g. the 'Terralift'). Although such devices have not, at the time of writing, been extensively evaluated, it is claimed that the soil fissures which they produce can act as channels for healthy root growth.

Apart from compaction, a frequent consequence of civil engineering work is an alteration in the movement of water, either as surface run-off or as percolating groundwater. If a newly paved or tarmac-covered area diverts the flow of rainwater so that the roots of existing trees receive too much or too little, it might be possible to correct this by altering the slope or providing seepage points. It must, however, be stressed that drainage problems can be hard to deal with on sites where established trees are present, especially where there is a need to dig trenches, thus risking further injury to the root system. It is also possible to correct nutrient deficiencies, but it should be noted that fertilisation can alter the susceptibility of trees to diseases, and that it can also induce imbalances if done inappropriately. It is therefore advisable first to find out whether an imbalance or deficiency exists by carrying out a foliar nutrient analysis.

One of the main benefits of being able to recognise poor site conditions and injury to trees during site development is that it can place landscape managers in a better position to guard against repeated damage of this sort. In many cases, approval for building developments has been given on the assurance that existing trees would be retained, but such assurance is worthless unless the trees and their growing conditions can be realistically protected. It may be helpful to consider three ways in which such protection could be exercised, although much depends on the adequacy of the relevant legislation and administrative procedures. First, if the plan itself seems incompatible with the proper protection of trees which have been selected for retention, this deficiency must be made known to all interested parties. Second, a scheme should be laid down whereby trees and their growing conditions will not be unacceptably damaged as a result of the development work or of projected use of the site. Third, there must be proper supervision to ensure compliance with the scheme.

Treatment of damaged or weakened trees

General considerations

The treatment of trees to control pests and diseases may help to avoid further serious attack, as discussed above. If a tree has already been damaged so that its structural soundness is affected, some form of surgery may be justified. This requirement only arises where the damaging agent has affected the main branches of a tree or shrub, or has interfered with anchorage as a result of extensive root dieback. Damage to leaves, young shoots or young roots is generally repaired naturally by the growth of new parts, and no treatment is appropriate, other than the maintenance of good growing conditions.

Damage to the permanent woody parts of the plant may sometimes have serious consequences for vascular function, structural support and visual amenity. The woody 'skeleton' can be damaged by anything which kills or removes an area of cambium, so preventing the normal formation of annual rings in the affected area. The damage may involve a physical injury, or a process of dieback or disease. Dieback may start in a branch and progress into the main stem, a process which may be initiated by a generally poor state of health. In many cases the damage starts on the main stem when an area of bark and cambium is killed by fungal or bacterial attack. If the attack is checked (either temporarily or permanently) by the tree's natural defences, the dead area becomes surrounded by new tissue (callus), derived from the living cells at its edge. The dead area is often described as a 'canker', although this term is sometimes not applied unless callus growth is present, giving rise to a roughened or raised appearance.

Cankers and physical injuries can provide a foothold for wood decay fungi. Sometimes the entry or growth of such fungi is facilitated by the galleries of wood-boring insects which enter the damaged part of the stem. Decay fungi have the ability to grow into wood and to use it as a food source, often virtually reducing mechanical strength to nil. Extensive decay in a tree can thus seriously weaken it. It is a general rule that the risk of decay increases with the area of cambium destroyed. This may be fairly restricted, for example where there is a single canker or an impact injury from a vehicle. If, however, the tree is under stress, a physical injury or diseased area may become the focus of much more extensive cambial dieback. An example is provided by the 'strip canker' which may occupy many metres along a stem and which may develop after a period of severe drought. Stress or localised disease may also result in dieback of entire individual branches or roots.

The nature of damage is also important; if an injury affects only the cambium and all tissues external to it, any resulting decay of the underlying wood will often be much less than that associated with a disease or other trauma (e.g. severe fire injury) which penetrates into the wood. For example, the partial debarking of beech trees by squirrels usually results in only a very restricted amount of wood staining or decay. The species of tree, the height up the stem, climate and the time of year of wounding are also important in determining the extent of decay associated with mechanical damage.

Injuries to a tree cannot, except to a very limited extent, be 'healed' in the way that healing can take place within the body of a mammal; i.e. by restoring structure and function in existing tissues. An injured area on a tree can, however, be occluded by the gradual over-growth of new wood and bark, starting around

PLATE 42
This stake is unnecessary and is causing serious damage to the tree.

its edges. The process of callusing sometimes results in total occlusion of the site of injury, and will then tend to arrest any decay which may have begun. This beneficial effect only operates when occlusion is complete, so that large or slowly callusing wounds or cankers remain open to attack by decay fungi for many years. Protective treatments have often been applied in the belief that they can act as an artificial callus, but there is no reliable evidence that currently available formulations have any such value in the long term.

The most important control of decay exists naturally within the tree in the form of physical and chemical barriers to the growth of decay fungi. Some of these barriers form in response to injury or infection, while others exist in the undamaged, healthy tree. The effectiveness of these barriers is determined by many factors, some of which relate to arboricultural practise. The advice given in this chapter and Chapter 10 is based on the need to carry out any surgical treatment in a way which promotes the formation of natural barriers and does not breach any that have already formed. Further information on the role of natural barriers in limiting the development of decay can be found in selected titles listed in the Further Reading at the end of this Handbook.

Treatment of fresh injuries

If the injured part consists of an area of debarked or bruised stem, it is occasionally possible to restore at least part of the damage by placing the bark in its original position and wrapping the stem with black plastic sheeting. Living cells at or near the separated surfaces may then be able to re-establish cohesion. Success is only likely if the bark has been merely loosened, rather than completely detached, and if the injury is very recent. This method is unlikely to work if bruising has been severe or if the injury has occurred outside the growing season. It may in any case fail with certain species, (e.g. *Fagus* and *Prunus* spp.). It should also be noted that some diffuse-porous broadleaved species and conifers can, due to the maintenance of sapwood function, occasionally survive ring-barking, although this will greatly reduce growth above the girdling point. Bridge-grafting can be used in such cases to help re-establish full vascular continuity.

If the surfaces exposed by an injury appear dry or discoloured, the time lapse has probably been too great to allow re-attachment of the bark, but it is still worth wrapping the

105

debarked stem with black plastic, since the exposed ends of the xylem rays may generate patches of callus which will grow across the wound, assisting occlusion. There is also some evidence that the exclusion of light can enhance the tree's ability to form internal barriers against invasion by decay fungi. Injuries exposed to strong sunshine or to heat reflected from paved areas should be additionally covered with some form of heat insulation.

Injuries which involve damage to the woody cylinder, as when trunks or branches are broken, can be occluded only by the growth of callus from around the edge of the breakage. This is a relatively slow process, so that a large wound may remain open to attack by decay fungi for many years. Quite apart from the problem that a large wound remains open to infection, the likelihood that the tree's internal defences will fail in the face of attack by decay fungi increases with wound size. There is no good evidence to support the view that the risk of invasion by such fungi can be reduced by the use of wound paints. Advice on this matter is given on p. 100 in connection with pruning.

If a branch has snapped leaving a long stub, it should be cut back to a natural major side-branch or, if none is present, to its base (see Figure 11.1). Branches which have 'broken out' from the main stem tend to leave the most untreatable wounds, but it is advisable to pare away any splintered wood and loose bark so as to provide a smooth surface on which fungal growth will not be unduly favoured. On no account should any work be done which would result in enlargement of a wound.

Wherever safety and aesthetic requirements allow, remedial treatments involving the removal of naturally broken or decaying branches should not be carried out on ancient parkland or common-land trees (especially pollards) since it might detract from their great value for dead-wood fauna and flora.

Root injuries often have very serious consequences for tree health, although they may be inconspicuous. Soil compaction by vehicles, the raising of soil level, and the alteration of drainage patterns can cause indirect injury, while the digging of trenches can sever much of a tree's root system. To say that prevention is better than cure would be an understatement, since there is very little that can be done to treat a badly severed root system other than to maintain or restore good growing conditions. It is, however, important to detect any immediate safety hazard which may have been caused by the resulting instability (see Figure 11.1).

Inspection and treatment of trees with old injuries

With time, attack by fungi, bacteria or insects may cause severely injured or stressed trees to decline in health or to become structurally weak. In particular, trees with badly damaged root systems may show a general deterioration, revealed first by a reduction in shoot growth and perhaps later by dieback in the crown. Progressive decline may be directly due to the root damage, to impairment of growing conditions, or to root rots triggered by the initial injury or stress. Such trees must be carefully inspected for any possible safety hazard, since their weakened roots may render them liable to windthrow. Crown reduction in the interests of public safety may be a short or medium-term alternative to felling, but the resulting disfigurement may detract from the amenity value of the trees concerned. Much of the amenity value of large, old trees is, however, bound up in the sentimental attachments of local people, which deserve to be seriously considered. Another role of old or ailing trees which needs to be considered alongside conventional arboricultural aims is their sustenance of a much threatened dead-wood fauna and flora.

Periodic safety inspections should also be carried out on trees which have or are suspected of having decay in the trunk or branches. Some knowledge of the patterns followed by the development of decay within trees will help in its detection, and expert advice is therefore often desirable. Increment borers (augers) are sometimes used for assessing the extent of decay, but there is some evidence that the damage which they cause can encourage the extension of decay into the surrounding sound wood. In many instances, a tree which shows sufficient external signs of decay to warrant such investigation is found to be already badly decayed. Narrow drill bits cause much less damage than augers. The drill hole can be probed along its length by a device such as the 'Shigometer' which measures the resistance to a pulsed DC current, or by a mechanical device which measures the compressibility of the wood surrounding the hole. Non-destructive techniques such as the use of ultrasound or X- or gamma-rays tend either to be impracticable for routine use or too inaccurate.

Like trees with weakened root systems, those with decayed main stems may have to be felled or subjected to crown thinning or 'reduction' in order to reduce the risk of breakage. Such action is not needed if there is a 'shell' of sound wood which is wide enough to give adequate structural support to the existing crown, but there is no precise mathematical definition of a safe width. It will depend on several factors, including the species of tree and the type of decay fungus involved. Expert advice is desirable wherever any doubt exists, but no-one is qualified to pronounce a tree to be completely safe, since exceptionally strong winds could snap or uproot any tree. In any case, the 'hazard rating' of a tree is largely dependent on its location with respect to roads, buildings and other vulnerable features.

For a tree in which a stem cavity has formed, the above considerations on hazard assessment and possible crown treatment apply, but there is the additional option of treating the cavity itself. It is very difficult to conduct research on possible treatments, but both observational data and a general knowledge of decay patterns suggest that some treatments do more harm than good. It seems particularly unwise to drain a water filled cavity, partly because drainage holes may encourage fungal invasion of the sound wood through which they pass, and partly because water which is permanently present in the bottom of a cavity probably inhibits decay by reducing the supply of oxygen to the decay fungus. Periodic wetting and drying-out may, however, promote decay by supplying both water and oxygen, and there is some interest in preventing this

by filling the cavity with a non-phytotoxic material.

Cavity fillings are much less often applied now than formerly. Little is known about their effects on the further development of decay, and they should not be used in the hope that they will control it. One possible justification for cavity filling has just been mentioned, and there may also be some value in the ability of a filling to encourage the closure of the cavity by directing the growth of callus across the opening, rather than into the cavity. This is likely to assist total occlusion. The value of assisting cavity closure is uncertain with regard to the structural strength of the tree. Removal of decayed wood from the walls of a cavity may also be useful, since it could be acting as a food-base for the decay fungus. However, no attempt should be made to carry this to the point of exposing sound wood, as advised in older textbooks, since this procedure could breach the tree's existing barriers to invasion.

If severe decay is present in individual branches, they can be cut back or removed. Similar action may be needed when a tree has developed mechanical weakness (with or without the presence of decay) due to the formation of breakage-prone branches or weak forks which should have been removed earlier in its life.

12 Buildings and trees

Rooting patterns

Many people still believe that the root system of a tree is some sort of mirror image of the crown. This can lead to misunderstanding of the nature of tree roots. Generally, major roots grow radially from the base of the stem within the top 30–50 cm of the soil, although there will often be some deeper roots both for feeding and anchorage. Roots which penetrate more than 150 cm below the surface, do so when the balance of moisture, oxygen and nutrients is suitable for root growth at that depth. In deep, freely draining sands or gravels, there may be two distinct layers of roots, an upper one taking advantage of surface moisture from precipitation, and a second layer deeper in the ground to exploit ground water during dry periods. The lateral extent of roots can be as much as 1.5 times the height of the tree.

Restriction of rooting can be caused by a number of factors; buildings, large areas of hard surface such as roads or car parks, impenetrable objects, waterlogged or compacted ground, competition with other vegetation. Some idea of root distribution may be obtained by extensive and costly root surveys involving boring and core examination. In practice, it is best simply to proceed with caution when working in the vicinity of existing trees until some idea of the extent of the root system becomes apparent.

A tree may have existed in a site for a hundred years or more, during which time the root and branch systems will have grown in a balance to allow healthy survival in the prevailing site conditions. Any sudden change of these conditions will upset that balance.

Development with existing trees

There are many actions and operations carried out by planners, architects, contractors and builders which cause tree damage or death, often because of lack of knowledge of the vulnerability of trees to even short-term changes. British Standard 5837 gives guidance on planning considerations where trees are involved and advice on avoidance of damage to trees by buildings and *vice versa*.

Site survey

It is wise to have a professional survey of the trees on a development site in order to define their current condition, estimate their span of useful life and obtain an idea of any maintenance work likely to be required.

Damage to trees by construction work

Root damage – soil level changes

At the outset, grading of a site can result in changes of soil level in the rooting zone of trees. Topsoil stripping, lowering or raising soil levels and compaction of soil, can all do harm by direct damage to roots or by modifying rooting conditions.

Root damage – compaction – seepage of toxic chemicals (see also Chapter 5)

Care should be taken not to compact the soil nor dump toxic materials below trees to be retained.

Root damage – trenching for services

Serious damage to tree roots often occurs when services are being laid in a building site. Assuming that the minimum spread of a tree's feeder roots, most of which will usually be located in the top 50 cm of soil, is probably 25% more than the crown diameter, it is possible to envisage the area from which building activities ought to be excluded and through which trenching for services should be carried out with extreme care. Once the presence of roots is detected when trenching, digging in that area should be by hand, leaving as many roots as possible

PLATE 43
Successful building development in existing woodland.

PLATES 44–45
Mature trees damaged by development. Root compaction is causing dieback and the trees are likely to become dangerous.

undamaged where they cross the trench. The services should be fed under the roots and the trench left open for the shortest possible time. Alternatively, it may be that some services can be 'thrust-bored', e.g. gas pipes or alkathene water pipes, thus requiring no trenching and causing minimal root damage.

Damage above ground – machinery

Large machinery used near trees frequently does serious direct physical damage to both branches and stems. This leaves ugly, mis-shapen crowns and wounds that are potential points of entry for pathogens that can have serious, long-term implications for tree survival and management.

Damage above ground – fire

Another common source of tree damage on construction sites is scorching of stems and lower crowns from fires burning too close to trees. This damage is frequently not visible until the dead bark becomes loose and falls away, often long after the contractors have left the site. Damaged trees may become colonised by pathogens and their lives drastically reduced.

Delayed damage

Mature trees rarely die suddenly, so the full extent of any construction site damage is not likely to become evident until long after the development has been completed. Death may then be attributed to a pathogen or a climatic factor such as drought. Once the development is completed and occupied, it is much more difficult and costly to maintain the trees in a safe condition.

Protection against construction damage

It is essential that trees worthy of retention should be fenced outside the drip-line of the crown in order to prevent damage. British Standard 5837 gives guidance on fencing to protect trees in this situation. There are sites where space is so limited that working within the root zone is unavoidable. On such sites it is advisable either to remove the trees and replant with smaller species of trees and shrubs when the construction work has been completed, or to bridge over roots to minimise damage where vehicular passage is inevitable.

Damage to buildings by trees

On residential sites a further problem is the suspected, actual or indirect damage to buildings by trees and the reaction of residents to mature trees near houses. Although purchasers are aware of the presence of trees when they buy their houses, and may know that there is a Tree Preservation Order in force which restricts any tree work that may be done without permission, it appears that many householders soon become 'anti-tree' people. They become very concerned about such things as autumn leaf fall and twigs, blocked gutters and drains, creaking or overhanging branches, restriction of light and infestation with aphids resulting in honeydew and sooty moulds. They then seek to have the trees removed, or at the very least lopped or drastically pruned, on the grounds that they are worried about the risk to their families and properties.

Subterranean damage

The principal form of damage that concerns property owners is that for which the cause is generally unseen and the onset is unpredictable. This is damage occurring to the foundations of buildings due to subsidence or heave which requires expensive excavation and underpinning to repair.

Subsidence damage is due to drying and shrinkage of the soil under the footings, which may create voids into which the foundations may subside. If this were to occur evenly over the whole area of the building, it would cause no problem, but shrinkage is usually differential resulting in cracking and settlement of different parts of the foundations to varying levels and possibly in damage to the building itself.

Even on shrinkable clays and peats, the risk of damage is avoidable with new constructions, provided adequate foundations are used as recommended by the National House Building Council, Supplement to Practice Note 3 (1985). British Standards, Building Research Establishment – Research Station Digests, and Codes of Practice should also be consulted. However, it is still common practice to use only the minimum strip foundation (75 cm or less deep) oblivious to the risks involved when building close to existing trees, particularly young trees. Furthermore, where no trees exist, there is always the chance that in future years they will be planted near to the building, resulting in removal of moisture, shrinkage of the soil and subsidence damage.

PLATE 46
It is not impossible for large trees and buildings to co-exist in close proximity. However, this is not recommended and eventual removal of an overmature tree in such a situation can prove hazardous and very costly.

Where a building is constructed near an existing mature tree on a shrinkable soil, the soil structure and therefore the foundations may be affected by the presence of the tree. When the tree dies or is felled, it stops removing moisture from the soil and the clay or peat then re-wets, swelling and upheaving the foundations and thus causing damage to the building fabric. Again, this can be avoided by the use of adequate foundations.

In periods of prolonged drought, such as occurred in southern Britain in the summers of 1975 and 1976, clays and peaty soils can dry and shrink sufficiently to cause subsidence damage even without the presence of trees. Obviously, adding trees that transpire freely in dry weather and extract vast amounts of moisture from the soil is likely to accelerate soil drying and increase the risk of damage.

There would seem to be a good case for determining the appropriate depth or type of foundation according to soil type on the assumption that trees will be planted or lost during the life of the building.

Physical pressure from the growth of tree roots is a very unlikely form of damage to buildings. Generally, conditions beneath a building are unfavourable for roots, unless there is a leakage of water from a damaged sewer pipe or water main, creating a moisture gradient along which roots could develop. Even if penetration beneath foundations does occur, a tree root can pass through a restricted section and expand again beyond the restriction. The pressure exerted by root diameter growth would not in any case be sufficient to lift a foundation on which a residential or heavier building is standing. Physical damage to structures is generally restricted to boundary walls on inadequate footings.

Stem diameter growth

When very large trees have been retained very close to a building (Plate 46) and roots and buttresses have been bridged to allow construction, damage has sometimes occurred due to lateral pressure on the foundations by diameter growth of the lower stem. If the problem becomes acute, the tree should be felled, and this may be a very hazardous operation (Plates 47–51).

38770

38772

38777

38779

38781

PLATES 47–51
Stages in the removal of a 70-year-old larch in a suburban garden at Sevenoaks.

New tree planting near existing buildings

When new trees are to be planted near to existing buildings situated on shrinkable clay or peat soils, and these buildings have been *in situ* for a number of years, there is likely to be no knowledge of foundation depth. In these situations it is a good idea to carry out a pilot excavation beside the building to determine foundation depth. Then, using NHBC Practice Note 3, tables and graphs, calculate a distance for planting from the building that would be safe, taking account of soil shrinkability, tree moisture demand and potential mature height.

Example

Tree to be planted   = Japanese cherry, mature height 9 m and moderate water demand.

Soil   = highly shrinkable clay (use Table 7[a] in Practice Note 3).

Foundation depth   = 1.0 m

For a foundation depth of 1.0 m and a moderate water demand broadleaved tree

D/H   = 0.7 where D = distance from building in metres and H = expected mature height in metres.

Therefore, D   = H × 0.7
       = 9 × 0.7
       = 6.3 m

Thus, the Japanese cherry should be planted at least 6.3 m from the building to counter the risk of subsidence damage.

Many older houses have cellars or basements, in which case the foundations would be likely to be 2.5–3.0 m below ground level and subsidence should not be a problem.

Where new development takes place and trees are planted in shrinkable soils around an estate, whether residential, industrial or commercial, one would expect present-day architects and developers to have enough knowledge of the problems of trees and buildings to ensure foundations are of sufficient depth to be without risk of damage from subsidence. Where it is evident that foundations are not adequate, trees and maybe shrubs would have to be planted at appropriately greater distances from buildings.

Incidental damage to trees

Stacking materials within the root zone is a common cause of dieback of garden trees, but probably the most common is the compost heap. These are often tucked out of the way under a big old tree, and can totally de-oxygenate the soil causing root death and 'stag-headedness' in the crown. Even just dumping grass clippings in summer or dead leaves in autumn can have the same effect.

Toxic chemicals used in and around the garden can cause problems. Preservatives splashed on trees or shrubs when garages or garden sheds are treated have done serious damage. Similarly, splashing of some exterior treatments to houses has caused death of trees and shrubs.

Careless use of certain herbicides can affect trees through the roots, particularly on porous, sandy soils or dry, cracked clays. Some herbicides volatilise easily and if they are applied under trees on still, hot days, the vapours can cause defoliation. Very careful reading of product labels is essential to make sure that the material is suitable and permitted for the intended use. It is now an offence to use chemicals for purposes for which no approval has been given.

Perhaps one of the more surprising possible causes of damage to small trees and shrubs is fencing. New galvanized wire netting used near small trees and shrubs can cause death due to zinc toxicity. Zinc may become dissolved in rainwater falling on the netting and be carried in solution to the tree or shrub roots. This is an unusual form of damage, because even 'new' netting has usually been in storage long enough for the zinc plating to have oxidised when it does not appear to be so toxic to plants. The same damaging effect can result from new galvanized corrugated iron roofs shedding zinc solution in rainwater on to trees and shrubs below. While this form of damage is unusual, it is a possible risk to young trees and shrubs.

13   Managing existing woodlands

Introduction

In Britain there are numerous woodlands in and around towns and cities. They are predominantly broadleaved, usually small in size, and are often the most important natural amenity people enjoy near to their homes.

It is difficult to overestimate the contribution of many such urban woods to the built environment. As well as having some limited timber potential they confer one or more of the following benefits.

1. Visual relief – screen industrial and residential developments; break up uniform areas of suburbia; provide contrast to the straight lines and symmetry of built development.

2. Recreation – woodland is able to absorb large numbers of people and provide an environment for many kinds of recreational pursuits, e.g. walking, riding, and nature study.

3. Conservation – some urban woods are vestiges of large areas of woodland dating back to the Middle Ages and most provide a valuable habitat for an abundance of wildlife and plants.

4. Education – the urban woodland provides a rural and biological laboratory accessible to schools not able to make visits to the countryside.

5. Microclimate – woodlands reduce windspeeds and slightly increase relative humidities.

Because of their importance to the community many urban woods are in public ownership, many people are interested in their preservation, and thus any work carried out in them arouses much interest (see Chapter 3). Urban woods generate little income because there have been few opportunities to manage them for timber production and the enjoyment of such woods by the public has traditionally been free. Consequently, expenditure on urban woods tends to be the minimum needed to maintain their present woodland condition. Also such woodlands often form part of the outdoor recreation facilities avail-able in a locality and their management tends to be overshadowed by that of parks, greens and recreation fields. Within the context of their many roles this chapter seeks to provide guidelines for positive management of urban woods.

The special features of urban woods

Urban woods present a number of challenges and opportunities for the manager which strongly influence silvicultural practices and how particular objectives are achieved. It is important to examine these first before recommending prescriptions.

Fragility

Many of the problems in managing urban woods directly reflect man's activities in or around them. But in addition, their small size, often old age, and frequently past neglect, bring special difficulties which make the woodland fragile, i.e. it will often not respond well to opening up by thinning, the remaining trees being vulnerable owing to overstocked condition, whippy stems, poor form, decay, etc.

Small size

In small woods, e.g. less than 1.0 ha, it is difficult to phase regeneration operations or to confine them only to one part. In small amenity woods a decision may be between clear felling and replanting or postponing the decision and prolonging the life of increasingly ancient trees. Postponement brings problems associated with neglect.

Age

As trees in a wood become older their contribution as an amenity usually increases, although eventually the need for regeneration has to be met. But old trees do not readily respond

PLATES 52–54
Urban forestry in the city of Leeds.

to change, many have poor coppicing ability, produce little seed and are prone to disease and dieback. Attempts to improve old woodland are often counter-productive and this is a particular problem in even-aged stands where all the trees mature at the same time. Many smaller urban woodlands fall into this category, thus, as early as possible, management should aim to produce a range of age classes.

Neglect

Active management of many urban woods has not been practised for decades and interest in them only resumed in the last few years. The main effects of neglect are failure to provide for or anticipate regeneration, storing rather than cutting of coppice, (i.e. growing on coppice stems to large size), overmaturity of many trees and a high stocking of tall, whippy stems with narrow, poor crowns. If gradual opening is attempted and a coherent canopy is broken, instead of responding to thinning many stands will 'collapse', stems snap, decayed branches fall and crown dieback sets in.

Pollution

The location of urban woods often exposes them to airborne pollution (dust, sulphur dioxide, exhaust fumes near roads) and to use as a dumping ground for rubbish. Narrow strips of 'ribbon' woodland beside roads or industrial or housing estates are particularly susceptible. These kinds of pollution can damage the health of older trees and harm regeneration.

Vandalism

Urban woods are marvellous places for youngsters to play, but inevitably damage occurs, though most of it is not usually malicious. Breaking branches or carving names, though unsightly, are only of minor consequence, but damage to young trees and saplings – uprooting, breaking, stripping bark – can prevent efforts at effective regeneration whether natural or planted.

People pressure

When a wood is popular and enjoyed by many, several kinds of damage can occur:

> wear and tear of tracks and paths often leading to localised erosion;

compaction of soil around prominent features, e.g. a noteworthy tree;

theft of plants, holly, Christmas trees, etc.;

disturbance of wildlife;

walking and trampling over young seedlings and other plants;

accidental fires.

Safety and security

Old trees become decayed, while trunks and branches may have structural weaknesses all of which can cause failure, particularly in stormy weather.

Liability of tree owners

Where a tree shows external evidence of decay or structural weakness the owner of the land on which it stands is normally liable for any damage it causes by breaking or falling. The Courts expect owners to inspect their trees regularly and obtain specialist guidance on interpretation of symptoms and assessment of tree safety.

Note: With certain exceptions it is an offence to fell trees without first having obtained a Felling Licence from the Forestry Commission. Additionally, where a tree is covered by a Tree Preservation Order issued by a local authority it will be necessary to obtain the prior consent of that authority before any lopping, topping or felling is carried out.

Management plans

The value of preparing management plans for new schemes has already been highlighted and often preparing plans of this type is also the best way of deciding how to care for existing woodlands. Such a plan has four ingredients:

1. assessing and recording woodland condition – size, age, species, public use, landscape and conservation value, etc.;

2. deciding and setting down objectives for each woodland – mainly a matter of setting priorities between, for example, visual importance, recreational value, timber potential, etc.;

3. identifying and drawing up work programmes needed (a) to satisfy the main objective, and (b) to ensure the general health

and well-being of the woodland in question, with schedules and budgets for the programmes;

4. making provision for regular review of progress and how well objectives are being met or specific projects implemented.

Even a simple plan can help to avoid inefficiency and poor results.

Woodland maintenance

Amount of use

In seeking to manage an existing urban woodland the first step is to determine the amount of public use. Most silvicultural problems relate directly to usage and woods should be classified according to this. For large woods an attempt should be made to zone areas according to different degrees of usage. Once these steps have been taken priorities can be accorded and a reasonable attempt made to apply a suitable silviculture.

Visitor surveys are not usually necessary to obtain information about use of an urban wood. Simple inspection will show where most people go and, obviously, car parks and rights-of-way indicate where the main public use is likely to occur. The pattern and degree of use may change following management.

Four categories describing degrees of usage can be conveniently identified; they are listed in ascending order:

A. little visited (fewer than 100 people/ha/year) owing to poor access, type of woodland, etc.;

B. moderately used (100–1000 people/ha/year). Mainly visited by those enjoying longer walks or wanting to undertake special studies, sport, etc.;

C. well used (1000–10 000 people/ha/year). Commonly areas of woodland within 100–200 m of a public road or car park;

D. heavily used (more than 10 000 people/ha/year). Mainly the edge of woodlands beside car parks and near to housing estates.

Not all woods will have every category. In particular, only large woodlands may have zones which fall into category A.

The overriding silvicultural need in most urban woods is to maintain and perpetuate tree cover. These aspects of management are considered for each zone category, but first it is important to outline some general principles in handling the woods and the people who enjoy using them.

General principles

The public generally have little knowledge of woodland management or experience of silvicultural operations, although they quite often have sympathy with conservation aspects. However, most people are happy to see operations which will help perpetuate the woodland they enjoy. Indeed, the foundation of successful silviculture is local support and encouragement: making the urban wood the community wood (see Chapters 3 and 4).

The following principles flow from what has been said.

1. Encourage good relations between owners/managers and the public.

2. Publicise silvicultural intentions particularly among local residents' associations, conservation groups, etc., or even involve local people directly in management committees such as those for many National Trust woodlands.

3. Erect signs to warn of dangerous operations and, where appropriate, include on-site notices describing what is being done and why and/or make mention of it in the local press.

4. Most people only take short walks and usually prefer to follow a prescribed route or path for comfort and convenience, thus these should be carefully planned and maintained, especially in much visited parts and so that visitors are channelled away from danger.

5. Neatness or tidiness are not features of a woodland, indeed semi-natural regrowth is desirable because it has a 'wild' appearance, but rubbish and litter greatly detract from enjoyment of a wood and may engender a less caring attitude on the part of the visitor.

6. Some practices seem to attract damage and are especially vulnerable, most notably the planting of single trees in readily accessible open spaces.

7. Where fencing is necessary, e.g. around regeneration, chestnut palings are often the most suitable being difficult to climb over while retaining a natural appearance.

8. Opening the canopy can increase enjoyment by creating glade effects and more diverse wildlife habitats.

Silvicultural recommendations

In the recommendations below it is assumed that the public enjoy right of access to the whole wood.

ZONES IN CATEGORY A – LITTLE VISITED

In large urban woods where some parts are little visited opportunity can be taken to pursue normal silvicultural practices to produce timber such as described in Forestry Commission Handbook 6 *Forestry practice* and Bulletin 62 *Silviculture of broadleaved woodland*. This is generally only worthwhile if at least 10 ha can be set aside. Such areas are often best managed by reintroduction of coppicing on a regular cycle, e.g. 2 ha every 3–5 years, where this has been practised in the past. For reasons of safety, thinning or felling operations should be confined to the winter when few visitors are expected. Areas of regeneration should be enclosed and paths and ditches should be kept clean and open.

Consider using part of this area for nature study/education or for a specific recreational activity. Also, in the very long-term, consideration can be given to bringing parts of Category A areas into greater public use to relieve pressure on parts of a wood in Categories C or D.

ZONES IN CATEGORY B – MODERATELY USED

Where there is moderate use of woodland by the public some yield of timber is feasible from thinnings to maintain stand health and from regeneration operations. If the size and structure of the woodland permits, felling and coppicing should be done in small areas, up to 0.5 ha, and fenced if necessary.

ZONES IN CATEGORY C – WELL USED

Where a woodland is well used the matter of public safety becomes especially important. Felling operations should initially be limited to the removal of unsafe trees. Where large gaps occur – a diameter of at least 1½ times adjacent tree height with as much sky exposed – they can be used for regeneration by accepting any naturally occurring seedlings or planting small groups of individually protected trees near the centre. Often satisfactory regeneration will come up in a thicket of brambles and other undergrowth; such areas should be encouraged and not cleared. Protection with treeshelters or similar guards will be needed if rabbits or deer abound.

Directly influence public enjoyment of the wood by making paths obvious, keeping them open and providing an all-weather surface. Consider having a circular route through the area which, if containing items of special interest, could be waymarked.

ZONES IN CATEGORY D – HEAVILY USED

Usually only small parts of a wood will experience very high use but in these personal safety must be of paramount importance. Remove decayed branches and fell unsafe trees (see Category C above). Plant in gaps by enrichment using individually protected trees. On occasions there may be benefit in planting standard or half-standard trees.

Consider providing public facilities such as car parks, toilets, paths, picnic areas and litter baskets. Also, consider in the very long-term relieving pressure on Zone D areas, particularly if regeneration is proving difficult, by establishing new facilities elsewhere in the wood.

The Potential for Timber

There are many urban woodlands which are of poor quality, over-aged and overstocked.
An important part of the future management of these woodlands will involve thinning and felling.
Timber from these operations will often be of low value. However, with care and skill this material
can generate revenue which can be used to offset costs of regenerating trees and woodlands.

14 Timber from urban forests

The harvesting of trees and woodlands which have had little or no management for very many years all too often demonstrates that decades of growth have only produced mining timber and firewood. Careful examination of the soil and site conditions frequently shows that, had the woodland been properly managed, it would have produced high grade timber while still providing the benefits of landscape, recreation and wildlife habitat. Often, poor quality timber results from an incorrect choice of species for the site, or the wrong mix of species. It is sadly true that practically anyone can grow poor quality trees. What urban forestry must aim for is high standards in silviculture and arboriculture which will, where appropriate, produce valuable timber.

While every opportunity should be sought for community involvement in urban forestry, the potentially hazardous nature of harvesting operations must mean that it will seldom be possible to encourage unskilled voluntary assistance. In most circumstances timber operations will therefore need to be carried out by trained employees, timber merchants or contractors.

Selling trees

Faced with the mixture of qualities and quantities predominantly available at present, the urban forester has to find a way of marketing these to the best financial advantage. These are the options:

>   trees sold standing,
>   trees sold felled (usually at road or ride side),
>   fell and convert for own use or sale,
>   chipping of lop and top,
>   firewood market for branch wood and other low quality material.

Trees sold standing

Provided the marking of the trees to be removed is done by a competent forester, who will take into account the objects of management, the standing sale is perhaps the best and most convenient option. The success of the sale will depend upon several factors.

QUALITY

It is always easier to sell high quality trees. That is trees which are large, straight and not diseased.

QUANTITY

Larger parcels are more attractive than small ones. A lorry load of timber, approximately 20 tonnes (roughly 20 cubic metres) is usually the minimum quantity that will interest a merchant.

ACCESS

Nothing hinders a sale more than difficulties in extracting the timber.

MARKETABILITY

Will the merchant be able to find an outlet for the timber?

A buyer of standing timber will have to allow for possible defects which may not be visible, e.g. shake in oak and chestnut, discolouration in beech and ash, internal rot (not always apparent from the outside), and healed wounds. Time of felling can affect the quality and therefore value of trees, for instance good sycamore is best felled between October and the beginning of December and quality ash should not be felled in early and mid-summer.

Timber sold felled

When timber is cut down the quality can be more readily ascertained. The presence or absence of shake, rot, unwanted colour and other determinants will all be made clear. However, the buyer will be aware that most timbers have to be removed from the felling site fairly quickly before deterioration sets in, particularly sap and fungal stain. The exceptions are oak and sweet chestnut which can be stored for long periods without deterioration. When felled trees are of poor quality the markets available are very limited: usually mining timber, chipwood for board making, cheap fencing and firewood. Prices from these markets may vary with species and size and so grading may have to be done. Sale to these markets is usually measured by the tonne over a public weighbridge.

Where the quality is better it may be worthwhile to make enquiries about the sizes (especially lengths), required by the sawmillers. Sawlogs are usually sold by the cubic metre, but a number of round timber merchants still buy on the Hoppus measure and this can lead to confusion. It will be to everyone's advantage to keep to the metric system for all measuring purposes.

If the felling is in small parcels of good quality, it may be worth bringing the timber to a central point and then grading it into separate lots for sale. There are still merchants who will be prepared to come and buy odd butt lengths of various species, subject to quality and price. Where an exceptional butt is available such as walnut or particularly dark oak or sycamore or oak of veneer quality, then care must be taken to avoid damage during felling operations, and in the case of walnut it may be better to dig out with root intact. In these cases it will be wise before felling to contact the firms who specialise in quality timbers and to remember that presentation of the timber is very important in achieving a good sale.

Competitive sale

Whether trees are sold standing or felled it is always desirable to ensure as far as possible that the sale is made on a competitive basis, as this is usually the only means by which the seller can discover the market value of his timber. Simple and relatively inexpensive advertisements in local newspapers are often all that is required to obtain a range of offers. It is also desirable to draw up a contract of sale which contains all aspects of the operation from commencement to completion of work, re-instatement of the site, method of payment, etc.

Utilisation

Few urban foresters will have the opportunity to deal in high quality timber and most will be faced with large quantities of mixed and poorly grown material. In order to market this it is worthwhile looking for new uses and outlets for timber in urban situations and opportunities to move into markets which traditionally have used expensive imported hardwoods. The following list indicates some of the possibilities.

1. Various types of fencing can utilise hardwoods making posts, rails, palings and panels, however it must be noted that most hardwoods will require treatment against rot.
2. Bollards for car park boundaries, play areas, site demarcation, walk way markers, orienteering courses, etc.
3. Plant tubs and containers. There is a big demand for these in various shapes and sizes and after suitable treatment against rot, most if not all broadleaved timbers, can be used.
4. Logs for playgrounds, play areas and parks, cut into special shapes or left in the round.
5. Edging for footpaths and walkways.
6. Timber blocks and chocks for use when using civil engineering plant and machinery.
7. Wooden litter bins. Many designs can use hardwood timber in short lengths.
8. Tree guards. There is a regular demand for these.
9. Gates. From farm estate and field gates to simple house gates, this is an increasing market where many types of timber can be utilised.
10. Seats and benches. Variation is endless and demand continues to grow.

Fell and convert for own use or sale

Very often markets such as those outlined above are unsatisfied, not because the suitable raw material is lacking, but because no means exist locally for converting timber for the specialised markets. In these circumstances people engaged in urban forestry, whether in local authority or in private enterprise, may wish to consider setting up a small sawmill. However, setting up

38758

PLATE 55
Furniture produced from urban trees;
Leeds City Council.

38724

PLATE 56
Cleft oak fencing.

a sawmill is an expensive venture and a great deal of research and planning will be required if the enterprise is to be cost effective. These considerations will include the following points of action.

1. A survey of available timber, detailing quantities, sizes and species and with a forecast of future availability.

2. A survey of local demand studying local markets and outlets with estimates of the diversity of material likely to be required and including possibilities for future market expansion, both in size and range.

3. Survey of possible sites with special reference to possible planning problems, access for large vehicles in all weather, and availability of storage space.

4. A review of possible building requirements including stores and offices.

5. An appraisal of sawmill machinery and equipment necessary for converting available timber to saleable products. Within this study may be included items such as joinery equipment, a kiln for drying and a unit for chemical treatment.

6. A study of possible sources for finance. Officers in the public service will be required to make a detailed investment appraisal for the entire project.

7. At the planning stage it will be wise to outline the financial control system envisaged, incorporating budgeting for quantity and cost, and with targets for output and surplus (profit).

Common difficulties

It is true to say as a rule of thumb, that the small mill should try to concentrate its effort within a small range. The more diverse the activities in a small mill the more difficult it will be to manage and to be efficient and viable.

As a general guide the minimum requirement is for a breakdown saw which is capable of converting all the log sizes available and a re-saw which will work quickly to accurate dimensions over a range of lengths. Smaller saws can be added if required.

In many situations the setting-up of a permanent sawmill will be financially unacceptable. In these cases it may be well worth considering mobile saws which can be transported to site where they will convert the timber. Machines have been developed which give reliable and continuous accurate sawing, producing well finished material. Some are capable of handling and converting logs of up to 100 cm in diameter and 6 m in length. They take the form of either high speed circular saws with moving beds or band mills which can be either vertical or horizontal. Each type has its merits and drawbacks. Before buying such a machine, time should be taken to see one in action and talk to engineers who understand the problems you are faced with, and who can advise on the best type of machine for the timber you are working with and for the type of finished article you wish to produce.

Whatever type of conversion you may decide on, waste is likely to be an important factor. The aim must be to utilise as much of each log as possible, provided that the marginal cost of dealing with the waste material does not exceed its value. Rougher lengths and heavy limbs can be dealt with by selling for firewood, for which there is usually a ready market in urban areas. The options for firewood sale are as follows.

1. Sell unconverted in full length to a firewood merchant at a price per tonne over a public weighbridge.

2. Cut the timber into short lengths around 2.5 m long. Many firewood merchants still buy the cord which is a stack of round timber 2.4 m × 1.2 m × 1.2 m. The solid measure of the stack will be 70% of its overall volume.

3. Convert into small log (firewood) size and sell directly to the user or to a middle man by the tonne or bag.

Chipping

Much of the lop and top from harvesting operations can be converted on site into wood chips for which there is a steady demand. The uses are:

footpaths – both public and private (e.g. golf courses),
children's play areas,
equestrian purposes,
fuel for wood burning systems (industrial rather than domestic),
compost and mulching.

There are many chipping machines on the market, both tractor mounted and self-contained units. Most chippers produce chips of various sizes from 4 mm up to 25 mm and more. For most purposes these are ideal. However, chips produced for fuel will need to be of a constant size if there is a worm feed into

PLATE 57
Wooden play furniture and bark chips;
Gosforth, Tyne and Wear.

PLATE 58
Fencing materials being produced from
urban timber; Leeds City Council.

the boiler. This is a critical requirement and if chips are to be produced for this purpose it will be necessary to ensure that the machine which it is proposed to purchase can reliably produce the required chip dimensions.

Chipping is often cost effective because cost associated with leaving lop and top in urban woodlands can be high in terms of fire risk and general untidyness leading to vandalism. If there is no ready sale for chips, then an option is to blow the chips straight back on to the woodland floor as a compost.

Very large scale chipping is done at mills where panelboard is produced from home grown and imported timber. Some of these mills may be interested in purchasing a regular supply of roundwood from urban forestry operations. Most hardwood timber is acceptable but poplar has to be kept separate, as it commands a lower price. Conifers are also very suitable for this market. Transport costs may tip the balance against selling to this market but if a panelboard mill has been set up locally then discussion with a buyer for the firm will be time well spent.

Timber treatment

If the aim is to produce sawn timber suitable for exterior use, to be sold direct to the user markets, then the timber will have to be treated with preservative to ensure durability. The provision of a plant for treating material represents a large investment and is a very specialised business. Unfortunately a great deal of timber is not properly dried before treatment and this results in a short life expectancy. If the appropriate British Standard Certificate is to be issued the pre-treated timber should have a moisture content of not more than 28% and this is difficult to achieve without long periods of stacking for drying, and drying kilns have to be considered as a means of artificially drying the timber in a short span of time without degrade. It should be made clear that treatment units and kilns are not luxury items of plant, they are the principal means of putting timber to uses which are outside the standard capability for many species, mostly on account of their short life span in outdoor situations. Nevertheless, kilning and chemical treatment of timber are specialist operations requiring technical knowledge and a sizeable amount of investment. It is beyond the scope of this Handbook to do more than indicate their potential value in the utilisation of produce from urban woodlands.

T. Exley

PLATE 59
Wood chips from urban trees being used to fuel a boiler heating 2 acres of glasshouses; Leeds City Council.

T. Exley

PLATE 60
Chipping on site to clear lop and top; Leeds City Council.

It will quite often be the case that the setting up of a successful enterprise to exploit material resulting from urban forestry operations is beyond the financial resources of one local authority, company or individual. A successful alternative strategy may lie in a co-operative system with several parties in an area getting together either to pool resources or to achieve economies by paying for contract work to be done on behalf of the group. There is also the option of appointing by contract or by employment, someone to market produce from thinnings and fellings with a brief requiring them to exploit local demand, secure orders, arrange contracts and supervise quality and delivery.

Footnote

This chapter has attempted to highlight some ways and further possibilities for dealing with types of harvested material familiar to most people involved in urban woodlands. As a footnote it is worth emphasising that the cost involved in harvesting and utilising low quality material will be much the same if not more than that involved in producing high quality timber. It is important therefore to ensure that the timber quality in urban woodlands is improved at every opportunity and to obtain the maximum income from timber operations. That income can be used to offset the cost of establishing woodlands of greater diversity and potentially greater wealth to be inherited by future generations.

Further Information

1 Contracts

The substantial benefits to be obtained from involving local community and other voluntary effort in urban forestry schemes have been described in Chapters 3 and 4. However, some types of work, especially operations such as tree surgery, felling and the use of heavy machinery, demand high levels of skill if essential safety and quality requirements are to be met. These services are usually only available from the employment of direct labour or contract services.

There can be strong arguments in favour of employing some direct labour. It can be particularly efficient in scattered or small scale operations where the cost and effort in preparing contracts is disproportionately high. A permanent labour force will be familiar with the areas involved and the operational requirements. In many circumstances a small experienced direct labour force will require much less supervision than contract workers.

Direct labour is nevertheless expensive to keep employed throughout the year when many tasks are seasonal and the overheads involved in procuring and maintaining the range of tools, transport and other machinery to cover a wide variety of tasks can be so high as to be unacceptable.

Contract work

When a contract is entered into, a number of basic assumptions are made by the parties to the contract. These include the following essentials.

1. The quantities involved will be clearly stated by the employer and the work will be fully carried out by the contractor.

2. Requirements for the quality of work, including safety requirements in its execution, will be clearly stated by the employer and carried out adequately by the contractor.

3. The contract time specifications are realistic and will be met by the contractor.

4. The cost of the contract has been arrived at fairly, it realistically reflects current costs and profit margins and the contractor can expect full payment on completion of the work or at specified intervals during the contract.

5. The contractor will indemnify the employer for damage caused by him or his employees during the course of the contract.

A properly constructed contract will provide the basis of mutual satisfaction for both parties. However, problems frequently occur when the quantity, quality and timing specifications of the contract are inadequately described and when insufficient care is taken to ensure that the price truly reflects the current market situation. It should also be borne in mind that effective supervision of the contract is an essential part of the transaction. Both the contract specifications and the supervision require professional expertise in forestry and/or arboriculture and management experience. Without such professional input, either from among the employer's staff, or from consultants, the prospects for a successful contract are very poor.

Even where work is 'free' because of the involvement of community or other voluntary effort, a clear specification for the work to be undertaken is still essential to success.

Site meetings

Whatever the form of the contract, and however small, it is nearly always advisable to arrange a site meeting with the prospective contractor(s) before the agreement is concluded, in order to ensure that the contract conditions are understood. The contractor will also benefit from such a meeting, as he will be able to explain problems arising from the draft specification and suggest suitable modifications which may be advantageous to him without prejudicing the interests of the employer.

Negotiated contracts

Many urban forestry contracts will appear small in comparison to civil engineering contracts, and it will often be the case that negotiating relatively small jobs with known and trusted contractors will be preferred by employers to the more difficult business of arranging for competitive tenders. The knowledge that a series of contracts will be available for negotiation will also help a contractor to plan in the medium and longer term to invest in capital equipment and to enter into financially advantageous commitments with his suppliers. Nevertheless, and despite these undoubted advantages, there are serious pitfalls which must be avoided. For example, if the contractor is already comfortably off for work he will be negotiating from a position of strength and it is all too easy for the employer to lose sight of changes in costs, and materials, and to rely on past experience rather than the latest market prices.

Competition

By inviting tenders for clearly specified work the employer can ensure that the resulting contracts adequately reflect the market availability of the resources he is seeking to employ, including a cost which fairly reflects the going rate. Invitation to tender can be open by means of advertisement in the forestry and arboricultural press, or closed by means of specific invitation to a limited number of known contractors. Open tender clearly offers the best opportunity for ensuring competition.

Where a number of contracts are likely to be needed because of large and diverse work programmes, the opportunity should be sought to offer a range of contracts to the market. Some could be small in size and cost and of short duration (for example a fencing contract or small planting scheme). Conversely, a tree maintenance and improvement programme for a large area might require a contract renewable over several years with a high commitment in terms of machinery and labour. By taking advantage of the normal variation in job size, it will be possible to encourage the development of a range of contractors – offering continuity to the large established firm, while allowing the small man to get a foot in the door at the small contract end of the market.

In the case of the larger contracts (especially maintenance contracts) there is always the danger of lack of precision both in the contract specification and in the supervision of the work. It is impossible to offer detailed advice in this Handbook on how to overcome this problem as each contract will be unique, reflecting the nature of the site and the tasks to be undertaken,

and any attempt to give broad brush prescriptions would only add to the imprecision which is to be avoided. It is essential that the schedules in the contract for arboricultural or silvicultural operations should be drawn up by a qualified tree officer. If this person is not available to the employer then a consultant should be employed to draw up the specification and if possible also to follow through by supervising the contract. It should be borne in mind that the arrangements with the consultant are also a form of contract and that the approach to employing a consultant should follow the same rules for competition and vetting as are recommended for employing contractors.

Even where a competent tree officer is available for drawing up contract specifications, it will still be desirable in the case of major contracts representing relatively large amounts of expenditure, for the contract to be handled by an experienced consultant. It is often extremely difficult to gain redress when a contract fails due to incorrect or imprecise specification, and so it will be cost effective to obtain professional guidance at the outset where the cost of failure is likely to be large.

In some cases consultants are themselves able to offer or arrange for contract services and some well established contractors also operate as consultants. Provided that care is taken to ensure that prices for the services are arrived at in competition, there is no reason why such combinations should not be employed, especially where large and complex schemes are being undertaken.

A model contract

The following example of a properly drawn up contract may be used as a model.

This agreement is made between (name of employer) (hereinafter called 'The Employer') and (name of individual and/or firm) of (full address) (hereinafter called 'The Contractor').

The contractor hereby agrees to carry out the work specified in the first schedule attached hereto, to the satisfaction of the employer subject to the following terms and conditions.

1. *Preliminary arrangements.* The employer will enable the contractor to commence prescribed operations on the dates scheduled and give him such instructions and advice as affect the contract.

2. *Work sites and access.* The contractor will familiarise himself with work sites and the authorised access routes. The use of such access routes shall be at the contractor's own risk and the employer shall not be responsible for any damage or injury arising out of the contractor's use of such routes.

3. *Payment.* The employer will pay the contractor the agreed price as detailed in the second schedule (attached) for the work specified in the first schedule (attached) provided that it has been completed to the employer's satisfaction. By mutual agreement payment may be made in instalments not in excess of the value of the work completed. 10% of sums due will be retained from all invoices to be paid on satisfactory completion of the contract. In the event of the contractor failing to complete any part of the work to the employer's satisfaction the employer may declare this agreement void (insofar as it relates to such part of the work), and payment shall only be made for any portion of that work certified as fit for payment. The contractor shall compensate the employer for any additional expenditure incurred as a result of his failure to complete the work satisfactorily.

4. *Liability.* The contractor will indemnify the employer against any claims for loss, injury or damage occasioned by the act of default of the contractor in the execution of this agreement, and will if so requested, satisfy the employer that he is adequately insured.

5. *Force Majeure.* In the event of any government regulation or departmental order coming into operation, or any act of God, strike, lockout or any other occurrence of a serious nature beyond the control of the contractor taking place, affecting their ability to perform their obligations under the agreement and as a result of which the work detailed in the First Schedule hereof is delayed or suspended, either party may request an alteration to the period of the agreement.

6. *Rewards.* The contractor shall not offer any reward perquisite or emolument whatsoever to any person in the employment of the employer.

7. *Health and Safety at Work Act 1974.* The contractor will accept full responsibility for compliance with the Health and Safety at Work etc. Act (1974), and all other relevant Acts and Regulations in respect of the work comprised in the contract and taking place within the land access routes or other premises of the employer. In the event of any breach of these standards commited by the contractor, subcontractor or nis employees or agents then he will be informed of the nature of the breach and of the remedial action to be taken within a specified time. Failure to meet the conditions imposed within the time specified shall be regarded as a breach of contract.

8. *Precautions.* The contractor shall take all reasonable precautions to prevent a nuisance or inconvenience to the owners tenants or occupiers of other properties and to the public generally.

9. *Assignation.* The contractor shall not sub-let or assign his rights under this contract except with the written consent of the employer and upon such terms as the employer may require.

10. *Suspension of work.* The contractor shall at the direction of the employer suspend or delay work on the whole or part of the contract, if in the opinion of the employer such suspension is necessary, and shall recommence such work within 3 days of the employers written order to do so. If in the opinion of the employer such suspension is due to circumstances which could not reasonably have been foreseen by the contractor, the employer may authorise re-imbursement of any increased cost which in their opinion the contractor has incurred.

11. *Termination.* If the contractor commits a serious breach of any of the terms or conditions of this contract, the employer shall have the right by written notice to require the contractor to remedy the matter within 14 days, and if the matter is not so remedied the employer shall have the right to terminate the contract, and any termination shall be without prejudice to the employer's other rights or remedies under the contract.

12. *Removal from site.* The contractor shall within 1 month of the termination of the contract remove from the site any equipment or erections belonging to him. Should the contractor fail to remove such equipment or erections within the time specified, the employer may retain or remove them as he thinks fit, and the contractor shall on demand re-imburse the employer for all costs incurred in their disposal after receiving credit for any value which the employer has placed upon them.

13. *Settlement of disputes.* If any dispute or difference of any kind shall arise out of any of the provisions of the contract

upon which agreement cannot be reached between the employer and the contractor, the dispute or difference shall be referred to an independent arbitrator agreed upon between the parties for a decision. Which decision shall be final and binding upon the parties.

Date:

Signed: Contractor:

Signed: On behalf of the employer:

Schedules

Each contract must be supported by a schedule detailing the operations to be carried out and giving specifications for the materials to be used. If appropriate, the schedule should make clear whether the materials are to be supplied by the contractor, the employer or by a third party. A second schedule will provide details of arrangements for payment. A map of the work site is essential, showing precise locations for the various operations, access for the contractor and his agents, any constraints on access or movement such as overhead electricity wires, underground water supplies and so-on, and indicating if appropriate where stores or other buildings may be located.

11 Useful addresses

Scientific or technical advisory services and grant aid or funding

Forestry Commission

Headquarters
231 Corstorphine Road, Edinburgh EH12 7AT

Forest Research Station
Alice Holt Lodge, Wrecclesham, Farnham, Surrey GU10 4LH
(Advisory Services and Publications)

Countryside Commission

England
John Dower House, Crescent Place, Cheltenham, Glos GL50 3RA

Scotland
Battleby, Redgorton, Perth PH1 3EW

Wales
Ladywell House, Newtown, Powys SY16 1RD

Department of the Environment
2 Marsham Street, London SW1 3EB
(Arboricultural Advisory and Information Service via Forestry
Commission Research Station, see p. 143)

Ministry of Agriculture, Fisheries and Food
Whitehall Place, London SW1A 2HH

Publications Office
Lion House, Alnwick, Northumberland NE66 2PF

ADAS (Agricultural Development and Advisory Service)
Block C, Government Buildings, Brooklands Avenue, Cambridge
CB2 2DR

DAFS (Department of Agriculture and Fisheries for Scotland)
Pentland House, 47 Robbs Loan, Edinburgh EH14 1SQ

WOAD (Welsh Office Department of Agriculture)
Cathays Park, Cardiff CF1 3NQ

DANI (Department of Agriculture for Northern Ireland)
Dundonald House, Newtownards Road, Belfast BT4 3SB

Nature Conservancy Council

England
Northminster House, Peterborough PE1 1UA

Scotland
12 Hope Terrace, Edinburgh EH9 2AS

Other information, advice and aid

Arboricultural Association
Ampfield House, Ampfield, Romsey, Hants SO51 9PA

British Trust for Conservation Volunteers
36 St Mary's Street, Wallingford, Oxfordshire OX10 0EU

Central Scotland Countryside Trust
Hillhouseridge Farm, Shottskirk Road, Shotts, Lanarkshire
ML7 4JS

Forest of London Trust
247 Pentonville Road, London N1 9NJ

Groundwork Foundation
Bennetts Court, 6 Bennetts Hill, Birmingham B2 5ST

Institute of Chartered Foresters
22 Walker Street, Edinburgh EH3 7HR

Landscape Institute
12 Carlton House Terrace, London SW1Y 5AH

Men of the Trees
Sandy Lane, Crawley Down, Crawley, West Sussex RH10 4HS

National Farmers' Union
Agriculture House, Knightsbridge SW1X 7NJ

National Small Woods Association
Unit 101, Butler's Wharf Business Centre, 45 Curlew Street, London SE1 2ND

Royal Forestry Society of England, Wales and Northern Ireland
102 High Street, Tring, Herts HP23 4AH

Royal Institution of Chartered Surveyors
12 Great George Street, London SW1P 3AD

Royal Scottish Forestry Society
11 Atholl Crescent, Edinburgh EH3 8HE

Royal Town Planning Institute
26 Portland Place, London W1N 4BE

Silvanus
Unit 4, The National School, St Thomas Hill, Launceston, Cornwall PL15 8BL

Scottish Development Agency (SDA)
120 Bothwell Street, Glasgow G1 2RN

Scottish Development Department
New St Andrew's House, St James Centre, Edinburgh EH1 3SZ

The Forestry Trust for Conservation and Education
The Old Estate Office, Englefield Road, Theale, Reading, Berks RG7 5DZ

The Tree Council
35 Belgrave Square, London SW1X 8QN

Think Green
Premier House, 43/8 New Street, Birmingham B2 4LJ

Timber Growers UK Ltd
Agriculture House, Knightsbridge, London SW1X 7NJ

UK 2000
London
2/3 Horse & Dolphin Yard, Macclesfield Street, London W1V 7LG
Scotland
c/o Esso Petroleum, Dunglas Bowling, Glasgow G60 5BH

Welsh Development Agency
Pearl House, PO Box 100, Greyfriars Road, Cardiff CF1 3XX

Woodland Trust
Autumn Park, Dysart Road, Grantham, Lincs NG31 6LL

III   The main diseases and pests of urban trees

The following pages contain a listing by tree genus of the principal diseases and pests likely to be encountered in urban plantings. Details of Forestry Commission and MAFF publications are given where appropriate. More detail can be found in *Diseases of forest and ornamental trees* by D.H. Phillips and D.A. Burdekin (Macmillan, 1982) and *Forest insects* by D. Bevan (Forestry Commission Handbook 1, 1987). Many of the disease problems are covered in *Diseases of trees and shrubs*, a superbly illustrated USA publication written by W.H. Sinclair, H.H. Lyon and W.T. Johnson (Cornell University Press, 1987).

BROADLEAVES

Alders (*Alnus*)
No major problems but limited available evidence suggests that *Phytophthora* root-killing could be a problem on sites subject to waterlogging (FC Arboricultural Leaflet 8).

Ash (*Fraxinus*)
The serious and largely unexplained dieback of *F. excelsior* that is so common in the countryside is not a problem in towns.

Some individuals of *F. excelsior* are liable to heavy cankering by the bacterium *Pseudomonas savastanoi* f. sp. *fraxini*. It is unlikely that such trees pose a threat to the health of others but they may be considered unsightly and not worth retaining.

Beech (*Fagus*)
Leaves of beech are commonly browned by the leaf miner *Rhynchaenus fagi*.

The beech woolly aphid *Phyllaphis fagi* occurs on the underside of the leaves. The combination of sticky honeydew and curled leaves can be a nuisance, especially on hedges.

The death of shoots, twigs and occasionally larger branches due to the action of the bark canker fungus *Nectria ditissima* is conspicuous in some years but calls for no control measures.

The stems of beech can be conspicuously infested with the beech coccus *Cryptococcus fagisuga* which in time can render them vulnerable to the bark killing fungus *Nectria coccinea* – the disease complex is known as beech bark disease (FC Bulletin 69). Removing or killing the insect prevents the condition from developing.

Beech is very much subject to bark stripping by grey squirrels.

The stem wood of beech is readily decayed by many fungi: pruning and other wounding should be avoided where possible. Several serious root-rotting diseases affect beech – usually in their later years – and kill them or render them unsafe. No preventive measures are known.

Birches (*Betula*)
In some years the leaves of birch commonly become spotted, yellowed and fall as a result either of infection by the fungi *Gloeosporium betulinum* or *Melampsoridium betulinum*. Fine twigs may also be killed. The lower part of the tree is often affected first.

Birch quite often bears 'witches' brooms' caused by the fungus *Taphrina betulina*. These have no adverse effect on the general health of the tree.

The wood of birch is quite perishable and subject to decay. In the south the most common cause is *Piptoporus betulinus*, a fungus which generally invades only damaged or weakened trees. In the north of Britain *Fomes fomentarius* is often encountered under similar circumstances.

Birch roots are very often attacked by honey fungus (FC Arboricultural Leaflet 2), and birch is the most susceptible of the commoner broadleaved trees to *Fomes* root rot (FC Leaflet 5).

Cherries and plums (*Prunus*)
In some years flowers and fruiting spurs may be killed by the fungus *Sclerotinia laxa*. The disease is sometimes so startling in appearance that it is mistaken for fireblight to which *Prunus* spp. are immune.

Shoot tips of cherry (*Prunus avium*) are often attacked by the cherry blackfly *Myzus cerasi* in early summer causing the soft new leaves to curl and the shoots to become stunted.

Silver leaf is an important disease of cherries and plums. Progressive killing of branches, and sometimes whole trees, occurs as a result of infection of fresh wounds by the fungus *Chondrostereum purpureum*. The wood is stained brown and the leaves may assume a silvery or leaden appearance.

A superficially similar disease, but characterised by the exudation of gum from the bark, is caused by the bacterium *Pseudomonas syringae* pv. *morsprunorum* (MAFF Leaflet 592). On *Prunus* 'Kanzan' an equally severe dieback occurs after severe winters: the cause is at present unknown.

Important root diseases include those caused by honey fungus (FC Arboricultural Leaflet 2) and *Phytophthora* (FC Arboricultural Leaflet 8).

Crab apples (*Malus*)
Some varieties suffer severe defoliation by apple scab caused by the fungus *Venturia inaequalis*. On the branches apple canker caused by *Nectria galligena* is occasionally a problem (see *Sorbus*).

Root killing by honey fungus is not uncommon (FC Arboricultural Leaflet 2).

False acacia (*Robinia*)
No particular problems.

Horse chestnut (*Aesculus*)
In some years leaves may show conspicuous yellow-bordered, chestnut-brown blotches in late summer due to infection by the fungus *Guignardia aesculi*. This has no significance for the tree's overall health. Other types of leaf damage such as interveinal and marginal browning or interveinal browning and tattering are not understood at present.

Occasionally in summer, partly severed, leafy twigs hang limply in the crown of the tree; some fall to the ground. They have been bitten through by squirrels which enjoy the young pith inside.

White woolly masses which appear in May on the trunks, especially of street trees surrounded by paving or tarmacadam, are females of the horse chestnut scale insect *Pulvinaria regalis*. The eggs laid beneath these scales hatch in June/July and the crawlers migrate to the leaves to feed by sucking sap.

Decay associated with pruning wounds is common but, in addition, the wood itself is quite brittle and branches are often broken by the wind without decay fungi being present.

Several serious root rot pathogens affect horse chestnut including honey fungus (FC Arboricultural Leaflet 2).

The cause of the abnormal proliferation of clusters of buds and short twigs on trunks and branches of the red horse chestnut (*A.* × *carnea*) is not known.

Laburnum (*Laburnum*)
Stem wounds and roots are liable to infection by the bracket fungus *Ganoderma adspersum* or *G. applanatum*. The trees may die as a result.

Phytophthora root killing can be a problem (FC Arboricultural Leaflet 8).

Limes (*Tilia*)
Certain limes, e.g. *T.* × *europaea* and *T. americana*, are liable to heavy leaf infestation by the lime leaf aphid *Eucallipterus tiliae* which produces abundant honeydew. This sticky deposit can be a serious nuisance on pavements, cars and public seats.

Premature browning in August of the leaves in the lower crown may be due to the lime mite *Eotetranychus tiliarium*, which later spins sheets of fine silk (like clingfilm) over the bole of the tree. Skeletonisation of the leaves is caused by larvae of slugworms (*Caliroa*).

The Caucasian lime (*Tilia* × *euchlora*) is subject to a bleeding stem canker of probable bacterial origin. The cankers, which may girdle stems, are usually near the branch bases and flux heavily in late summer. This disease is sufficiently common and severe to put in question the use of *T.* × *euchlora* in formal plantings. The scale insect *Pulvinaria regalis* occurs on stressed trees (see under Horse chestnut).

The limes are some of the more susceptible trees to *Phytophthora* root killing (FC Arboricultural Leaflet 8).

Maples (*Acer*) (see also sycamore)
Verticillium wilt (caused by the soil-borne fungus *V. dahliae*) can be a problem in young trees either in the nursery or, less commonly, at the planting site if infected trees are used. It occasionally also occurs in older trees (FC Arboricultural Leaflet 9).

Oaks (*Quercus*)

Defoliation of oaks by the larvae of several different moths may occur in May/June but the trees re-flush by July (DoE Arboriculture Research Note 60/88/ENT).

In some years leaves may be conspicuously discoloured by heavy infestation of the oak leaf phylloxera (*Phylloxera glabra*). Cynipid wasps are responsible for the production of a multitude of often pretty and quite harmless galls. Special mention should be made of the knopper gall *Andricus quercuscalicis* on the cupule of *Q. robur* which usually prevents development of the acorn (DoE Arboriculture Research Note 55/84/ENT).

Serious stem decay may be caused by the bracket fungus *Laetiporus sulphureus*. Older trees are liable to attack by several root rotting fungi, notably *Inonotus dryadeus* and several *Ganoderma* spp.

Pears (*Pyrus*) See Crab apples.

Plane (*Platanus*)

London plane (*P.* × *acerifolia*) is very susceptible to anthracnose caused by the fungus *Gnomonia errabunda* (= *G. platani*). This fungus can kill twigs or developing shoots or cause heavy early summer leaf fall. Recovery is usually quick and good (DoE Arboriculture Research Note 46/83/PATH).

On roadsides, the failure of buds to flush fully on certain branches may be due to damage from road de-icing salt (DoE Arboriculture Research Note 47/83/PATH).

The scale insect *Pulvinaria regalis* sometimes occurs on the trunk (see under Horse chestnut). The bracket fungus *Inonotus hispidus*, entering via pruning wounds, is quite commonly the cause of serious stem disease. Wood strength may be significantly reduced before much decay is evident.

London plane is one of the more resistant trees to honey fungus.

Plums (*Prunus*) See Cherries.

Poplars (*Populus*)

In some years the leaves of certain poplars commonly become spotted, blotched or discoloured by the fungi *Marssonina*, *Melampsora* or *Pollaccia*. The lower part of the tree is often the first to be affected and twig dieback sometimes ensues.

Brown patches on the leaves are also caused by the poplar leaf beetles *Phyllodecta vitellinae* and *P. vulgatissima*; both larvae and adults feed on the lower epidermis.

The stems, branches and twigs of many poplars (but not Lombardy) are commonly cankered and killed by the bacterium *Xanthomonas populi*. The cause of a common branch dieback of Lombardy poplar is unknown.

Rowans (*Sorbus aucuparia* group)

Green or brown pustule-like galls caused by the mite *Phytoptus sorbi* can cover rowan leaves, spoiling their appearance, but are not believed otherwise to harm the tree.

Rowans are often affected by *Nectria* canker disease which causes death of shoots and branchlets. Despite the conspicuous symptoms in certain years, no remedial action is called for. The common rowan is much less susceptible to fireblight, caused by the bacterium *Erwinia amylovora*, than are the whitebeams (*Sorbus aria* group), but this disease is severe on some of the other rowans (MAFF Leaflet 571).

Silver leaf, caused by the fungus *Chondrostereum purpureum*, occasionally causes branch death.

Rowan is quite susceptible to root killing by honey fungus.

Sweet chestnut (*Castanea*)

Pruning wounds are commonly invaded by the wood rotting fungus *Laetiporus sulphureus*.

On wet sites, roots are liable to be killed by *Phytophthora* (FC Arboricultural Leaflet 8). Trees may be killed but often show severe dieback and then eventually recover.

Sycamore (*Acer pseudoplatanus*)

Tar spot, caused by the fungus *Rhytisma acerina*, often disfigures sycamore leaves in sulphur dioxide-free atmospheres. It does not affect the general health of the tree. In addition, sycamore leaves may show a severe brown marginal scorch of unknown cause.

The sycamore leaf aphid (*Drepanosiphum platanoidis*) is often abundant on the leaves through spring and summer where it produces large quantities of honeydew. This sticky deposit may be a considerable nuisance on cars, pavements and public seats.

The scale insect *Pulvinaria regalis* occurs on the trunks of stressed trees (see under Horse chestnut).

Like other maples, sycamore in the nursery can suffer from *Verticillum* wilt (see Maples). Sycamore is exceedingly subject to bark stripping by grey squirrels. If girdling is complete, this results in dramatic browning of the foliage in mid-summer. Following very hot dry summers sycamore may suffer from sooty bark disease caused by the wood-invading fungus *Cryptostroma corticale* (FC Arboricultural Leaflet 3).

Sycamore is moderately susceptible to root killing by honey fungus (FC Arboricultural Leaflet 2).

Thorns (*Crataegus*)
In some years heavy leaf spotting and fall may result from infection by the fungus *Diplocarpon mespili*.

Defoliation of thorns and other rosaceous trees and shrubs in south-east England may be caused by the brown-tail moth *Euproctis chrysorrhoea* whose larvae have irritant hairs (DoE Arboriculture Research Note 57/85/EXT). Another hairy but non-irritant species, which occurs more widely on various trees, is the lackey (*Malacosoma neustria*). The young larvae of both species live gregariously in 'nests'. Small larvae feeding under swathes of silk are those of *Scythropia crataegella*, also found on cotoneaster.

Although fireblight, caused by the bacterium *Erwinia amylovora*, is quite common on hawthorn, trees are rarely killed (MAFF Leaflet 571).

Hawthorn seems to be relatively susceptible to killing by *Phytophthora* root disease (FC Arboricultural Leaflet 8).

Whitebeam (*Sorbus aria* group)
Whitebeam is among the most susceptible of all the ornamental trees to fireblight caused by the bacterium *Erwinia amylovora* (MAFF Leaflet 571) and infected trees are likely to die.

Whitebeam may be killed slowly by the root rotting fungi *Ganoderma adspersum* or *G. applanatum*.

Willows (*Salix*)
In some years, leaf cast and shoot and twig killing diseases seriously affect some of the common ornamental willows – notably *Salix alba* 'Tristis', *S. matsudana* 'Tortuosa' and *S. fragilis*. Some willow varieties are resistant to one or other of the fungal pathogens responsible (DoE Arboriculture Research Notes 78/89/PATH and 79/89/PATH).

Brown patches on leaves may be caused by leaf beetles (*Phyllodecta* spp.) (see under Poplars).

Certain cultivars of *Salix alba*, most notably the cricket bat willow, are very susceptible to the bacterium *Erwinia salicis* which infects the wood and causes a progressive dieback. Other types of willow are more resistant but any diseased trees should be destroyed in order to protect the bat willow industry. In some parts of the country the disease is controlled under the Watermark Disease of Willow (Local Authorities) Order (FC Leaflet 20).

Willows are very susceptible to root killing by honey fungus (FC Arboricultural Leaflet 2).

CONIFERS

Cedars (*Cedrus*)
Cedars can occasionally suffer a dieback due to the effects of the shoot aphid *Cedrobium laportei*, whose presence in May and June will be indicated by abundant honeydew dropping from the tree. This honeydew will later become colonised by black 'sooty moulds'.

Death of branchlets caused by the fungus *Potebniamyces coniferarum* is quite common on Deodar cedar.

Cedars are among the most susceptible of the conifers to killing by honey fungus.

Cypresses, false cypresses (*Chamaecyparis*)
Brown foliage and branch dieback, particularly on hedges, may be due to the aphid *Cinara cupressi* (see under Leyland cypress).

Lawson cypress is very susceptible to two usually fatal root diseases, honey fungus (FC Arboricultural Leaflet 2) and *Phytophthora* (FC Arboricultural Leaflet 8).

True cypresses (*Cupressus*)
Monterey cypress (*C. macrocarpa*), and Italian cypress (*C. sempervirens*) are very susceptible to the branch killing disease 'Coryneum canker' caused by the fungus *Seiridium cardinale*. In time the whole tree may die (DoE Arboriculture Research Note 39/88/PATH).

Leyland cypress (× *Cupressocyparis leylandii*)
In some years, infestation by the cypress aphid *Cinara cupressi* causes extensive leaf browning and death of branches. Often the damage is worse in the lower part of the tree (DoE Arboriculture Research Note 80/89/ENT).

Branch killing by *Coryneum* canker (see above) is becoming increasingly common in Leyland cypress, but the damage to the tree is less severe than on Monterey cypress.

Leyland cypress is very susceptible to killing by honey fungus

(FC Arboricultural Leaflet 2) but is very resistant to *Phytophthora* root disease.

Douglas fir (*Pseudotsuga*)
Severe distortion of needles and associated white waxy wool is caused by the Douglas fir woolly aphid *Adelges cooleyi*.

Japanese cedar (*Cryptomeria*)
No particular problems.

Junipers (*Juniperus*)
Some species, including *J. chinensis* and *J. virginiana* are susceptible to shoot damage caused by the aphid *Cinara fresai*; the cultivar *J. virginiana* 'Skyrocket' may be killed (DoE Arboriculture Research Note 80/89/ENT). Scale insects (*Carulaspis*) infest the leaves and cones. Needle mining and webbing in May/June is caused by the juniper webber moth *Dichomeris marginella*.

Larches (*Larix*)
Leaf infestation by the woolly aphid *Adelges laricis* can lead to severe dieback in susceptible provenances of European larch. The same provenances are susceptible to larch canker caused by the fungus *Trichoscyphella willkommii*. Larch is susceptible to *Fomes* butt rot caused by *Heterobasidion annosum* (FC Leaflet 5).

Monkey puzzle (*Araucaria*)
Trees may die through root killing by honey fungus (FC Arboricultural Leaflet 2).

Pines (*Pinus*)
In some years, severe needle discoloration and cast of 2-year-old and older needles may be caused by a number of fungal diseases. They are normally of little consequence for the future life of the tree.

Young pines may also suffer shoot and bud damage caused by larvae of the pine shoot moth *Rhyacionia buoliana* which can result in stem deformities. Also on young trees the aphid *Eulachnus agilis* causes loss of older needles and *Schizolachnus pineti* causes yellowing of current needles.

White waxy wool produced by the pine woolly aphid *Pineus pini* may be conspicuous on twigs and stems.

Spruces (*Picea*)
Foliage becomes yellow-banded early in the year, and then brown, due to the green spruce aphid *Elatobium abietinum*. Damage can be expected following mild winters. Bronzing of older needles associated with very fine silk is symptomatic of the conifer spinning mite *Oligonychus ununguis*. *P. pungens* var. *glauca* is particularly susceptible to both these pests.

Spruces are very susceptible to *Fomes* butt rot (FC Leaflet 5).

Thujas (*Thuja*)
No major problems, although older trees of western red cedar (*T. plicata*) are very susceptible to *Fomes* butt rot (FC Leaflet 5).

True or silver firs (*Abies*)
Shoots may be killed by infestations of the aphid *Adelges nordmanniana*.

North American species suffer from a stem colonising aphid, *Adelges piceae*, that causes crown dieback by impairing the water conducting ability of the wood.

Wellingtonia (*Sequoiadendron*)
The top several feet of this tree are commonly killed by lightning. Even when large it is quite susceptible to root killing by honey fungus (FC Arboricultural Leaflet 2).

Yew (*Taxus*)
Older needles yellow and fall prematurely in some years. An earlier drought is the likely cause. Bronzing or browning and death of needles may occur in particularly cold winters.

Shoots girdled by larvae of the moth *Ditula angustiorana* in late spring turn yellow and then die. This is sometimes particularly noticeable on fastigiate yews.

The only fatal disease is *Phytophthora* root disease to which yew is very susceptible (FC Arboricultural Leaflet 8).

Ancient trees are commonly badly decayed by the heart-rotting fungus *Laetiporus sulphureus*.

IV   Further reading

Forestry Commission publications

Bulletins

59	Seed manual for ornamental trees and shrubs, 1982	£5.00
62	Silviculture of broadleaved woodland, 1984	£9.50
65	Advances in practical arboriculture, 1987	£8.50
78	Natural regeneration of broadleaves, 1988	£3.00
80	Farm woodland planning, 1988	£6.95
09	Seed manual for commercial forestry species	(in press)

Booklets

15	Conifers (revised 1985)	£2.95
20	Broadleaves (revised 1985)	£3.95

Handbooks

2	Trees and Weeds – weed control for successful tree establishment, 1987	£2.70
3	Farm woodland practice, 1988	£7.50
6	Forestry practice	(in press)

Field Book

8	The use of herbicides in the forest, 1989	£4.00

Research and Development Papers

132	Reclamation of mineral workings to forestry, 1983	£1.50
136	Tree planting in colliery spoil, 1985	50p
141	A guide to the reclamation of mineral workings for forestry, 1985	£2.50

Arboriculture Research Notes

1/84/ARB	Control of conker formation
2/88/PATH	Breeding elms resistant to Dutch elm disease
5/87/WILD	Plastic mesh tree guards
8/79/ARB	Damage to broadleaved seedlings by desiccation
9/79/SILS	The clones of Leyland cypress
12/79/SILS	Summer branch drop
13/88/PATH	English elm regeneration
14/87/TV	The effect of trees on television reception
16/82/PATH	Decay and disintegration of dead elms
18/87/PATH	The detection of decay in trees with particular reference to the use of the Shigometer
20/82/PATH	Bacterial wetwood
21/88/SILS	Coppice
22/80/SILS	Root deformation by biodegradable containers
24/80/SILS	Tree roots and foundations
25/80/PATH	Canker stain of plane
27/88/SILS	Herbicides for sward control among broadleaved amenity trees
29/81/SILS	The native and exotic trees in Britain
33/81/EXT	The improvement of birch for forestry and amenity
35/81/SILN	Winter shelter for agricultural stock
36/85/TRL	Tree roots and underground pipes
37/84/SSS	Reclamation of surface workings for trees I. Landforms and cultivation
38/84/SSS	Reclamation of surface workings for trees II. Nitrogen nutrition
39/88/PATH	Coryneum canker of Monterey cypress and related trees
40/89/ARB	Tree staking
43/87/WILD	Rabbit control – phostoxin
44/83/SSS	The effects of tree species on vegetation and nutrient supply in lowland Britain
45/83/PATH	Cobweb fungus – Athelia
46/83/PATH	Anthracnose of London plane
47/83/PATH	Crown damage to London plane
48/83/PATH	A definition of the best pruning position
50/83/SSS	Nutrition of broadleaved amenity trees I. Foliar sampling and analysis for determining nutrient status
52/84/SSS	Nutrition of broadleaved amenity trees II. Fertilisers
53/88/WS	Chemical weeding: hand-held direct applicators
54/86/SILS	Control of epicormic shoots on amenity trees
55/84/ENT	The knopper gall

56/84/SEED	*Dormant tree seeds and their pre (sowing) treatment*
57/85/EXT	*The brown-tail moth*
58/87/PATH	*Phytophthora root disease*
59/87/ARB	*The effects of weed competition on tree establishment*
60/88/ENT	*Oak defoliation*
61/85/PATH	*Ceratotect – a fungicide treatment for Dutch elm disease*
63/87/SILS	*Treeshelters*
64/86/SILN	*Rough handling reduces the viability of planting stock*
65/86/SILS	*Alternatives to simazine for weed control in transplant lines and shrubberies at time of planting*
66/86/EXT	*Planting success rates – standard trees*
67/87/ARB	*A comparison of the survival and growth of transplants, whips and standards, with and without chemical weed control*
68/87/PAT	*Lightning damage to trees in Britain*
69/87/SILS	*Do soil ameliorants help tree establishment?*
70/87/SSS	*Surveys of tree health 1987*
71/87/ARB	*Black polythene mulches to aid tree establishment*
72/87/ARB	*Sheet mulches: suitable materials and how to use them*
73/87/PAT	*Treatment of storm-damaged trees*
74/87/ARB	*Protecting trees from field voles*
75/88/ARB	*Alginure root dip and tree establishment*
76/88/SSS	*Sewage sludge as a fertiliser in amenity and reclamation plantings*
77/89/ARB	*Stakes and ties*
78/89/PATH	*Marssonina canker and leaf spot (anthracnose) of weeping willow*
79/89/PATH	*Scab and black canker of willow*
80/89/ENT	*Cypress and juniper aphids*
81/89/ARB	*Ivy – boon or bane?*

Arboricultural Leaflets

1	*The external signs of decay in trees* (revised 1984)	£1.00
2	*Honey fungus* (revision expected)	
3	*Sooty bark disease of sycamore*, 1978	40p
4	*Virus and virus-like diseases of trees* (reprint expected)	
5	*Decay fungi in broadleaved trees*, 1980	£2.00
6	*Trees and water*, 1980	£2.00
7	*Removal of tree stumps*, 1981	£2.00
8	*Phytophthora diseases of trees and shrubs*, 1981	£2.40
9	*Verticillium wilt*, 1981	£1.35
10	*Individual tree protection*, 1985	£2.00

Educational publications

A forest adventure (Teachers' Pack)	One free per school
Teachers' pack (Westonbirt)	£2.00

Private woodland booklets (free)

Woodland grant scheme

Consultation procedures for forestry grants and felling permissions

Control of tree felling

Advice on establishment and tending of trees (with notes on choice of species) – a reprint of Chapter 3 from FC Bulletin 14 *Forestry practice* (10th edition)

Forest Industry Safety Guides (free)

The Safety Guides published by the Forestry Safety Council give a summary of safe working practices helping employees and employers to comply with the Health and Safety at Work etc. Act 1974. In many cases, an appropriate checklist is available for use by supervisors, safety officers, etc. at inspections. All are available free from the FC Publications Section or from The Secretary, Forestry Safety Council, 231 Corstorphine Road, Edinburgh EH12 7AT.

Miscellaneous

Decorative trees for country, town and garden, 1984 A.F. Mitchell and J. Jobling, HMSO	£9.95
Wood as fuel, 3rd edition, 1987	20p
The recognition of hazardous trees	Free
Forestry Commission catalogue of publications	Free

Occasional Papers

7	*Establishment of trees on regraded colliery spoil heaps*, 1980	£1.00
14	*The Gwent Small Woods Project 1979–84*, 1985	£3.50

Publications from other organisations

Protected trees – a guide to tree preservation procedures (DoE and Welsh Office)	Free

The Arboricultural Advisory and Information Service

Following recommendations made in 1974 by the Arboricultural Research Working Party, the Department of the Environment has established an Arboricultural Advisory and Information Service.

This service, which is located at the Forestry Commission Research Station, is staffed with specialist arboriculturists and draws on the expertise and facilities already existing within the Forestry Commission, other research stations and universities.

The service is designed to help professional arboriculturists in commercial practice, local authorities, landscape designers and plant producers. Other professions on the fringes of arboriculture also benefit from this service. Enquiries from private individuals are dealt with as far as resources permit.

Other publications

Planning, design and management

ALDOUS, T. (1988). *Inner city urban regeneration and good design.* HMSO, London. (32 pp.)

ANON. (1985). *Building near trees.* National House-Building Council, Practice Note 3.

ANON. (1985). *A quick way to find the right depth of foundations on clay soils.* National House-Building Council, Supplement to Practice Note 3.

ARBORICULTURAL ASSOCIATION (1988). *Tree survey and inspection* (compiled by D.R. Helliwell). (Copies are available, price £2.25, inc. post & packing, from the Secretary, Arboricultural Association, Ampfield House, Ampfield, Nr Romsey, Hants SO51 9PA).

ARBORICULTURAL ASSOCIATION. *Guide to tree planting.* A handout.

BRADSHAW, A.D., GOODE, D.A. AND THORP, E.H.P. (1983). *Ecology and design in landscape.* The 24th Symposium of the British Ecological Society, Manchester. Blackwell Scientific Publications, Oxford. (463 pp.)

BROOKER, R. AND CORDER, M. (1986). *Environmental economy.* E. & F. N. Spon Ltd., London. (224 pp.)

CHRISTIANSEN, M.L. (1983). *Vandalism control management for parks and recreation areas.* E. & F. N. Spon Ltd., London.

CIVIC TRUST (1988). *Environmental directory.* (National and regional organisations of interest to those concerned with amenity and the environment.) Civic Trust, 7th edtn. (69 pp.)

COUNTRYSIDE COMMISSION (1982). *Informal countryside recreation for disabled people.* Countryside Commission, Cheltenham. (Advisory Series No.15). (79 pp.)

COUNTRYSIDE COMMISSION (1986). *Recreation 2000. Enjoying the countryside: a consultation paper.* Countryside Commission, Cheltenham (CCP 225).

COUNTRYSIDE COMMISSION (1986). *Access to the countryside for recreation and sport.* Report to the Countryside Commission and the Sports Council by the Centre for Leisure Research. Countryside Commission, Cheltenham (CCP 217). (170 pp.)

COUNTRYSIDE COMMISSION (1986). *A directory of training opportunities in countryside conservation and recreation.* Countryside Commission, Cheltenham (CCP 138). (29 pp.)

CUTLER, D.F. AND RICHARDSON, I.B.K. (1981). *Tree roots and buildings,* based on *Kew tree root survey,* published by Construction Press.

DEPARTMENT OF THE ENVIRONMENT (1987). *Greening city sites.* HMSO, London. (127 pp.)

FYSON, A. (1983). *Education and participation.* In *City landscape,* 150–156. A contribution to the Council of Europe's campaign for urban renaissance. Butterworths, London.

GREY, G.W. AND DENEKE, F.J. (1986). *Urban forestry,* 2nd edition. J. Wiley & Sons, New York. (299 pp.)

HACKETT, B. (1983). *Opportunities in city landscape.* In *City landscape,* 1–9. A contribution to the Council of Europe's campaign for urban renaissance. Butterworths, London.

HART, C.E. (1986). *Private woodlands: a guide to British timber prices and forestry costings.* Published by the author, Coleford, Glos. (154 pp.)

HELLIWELL, D.R. (1985). *Trees on development sites.* Arboricultural Association. (18 pp.)

INSLEY, H. (1981). *Reducing establishment losses.* In 21st Askham Bryan Horticultural Technical Course 1981, pp. 32–38. Askham Bryan College of Agriculture and Horticulture, York.

LANCASHIRE COUNTY COUNCIL (1986). *Lancashire's woodland heritage.* An introduction based on the County. Lancashire County Council, Preston. (42 pp.)

MILLER, R.W. (1988). *Urban forestry: planning and managing urban greenspaces.* Prentice Hall, Englewood Cliffs, New Jersey, USA. (404 pp.)

PHILLIPS, A.F. AND GANGLOFF, D.J. (1987). *Proceedings of the 3rd National Urban Forestry Conference.* American Forestry Association, Washington. (327 pp.)

SYKES, J.M. AND BRIGGS, D.R. (1981). *An assessment of amenity tree planting schemes*. A report to the Countryside Commission by the Institute of Terrestrial Ecology (NERC). Countryside Commission, Manchester. (32 pp.)

THODAY, P.R. (ed.) (1983). *Tree establishment*. Proceedings of a Symposium held at the University of Bath on 14/15 July 1983. (78 pp.)

THODAY, P.R. AND KENDLE, A.D. (1988). *Tree establishment after the storm*. In Proceedings of a Conference *After the storm – one year on* held at St. Catherine's College, Oxford, 4 October 1988. The Tree Council, London.

Diseases and disorders

ANON. (1979). *Silver leaf disease of fruit trees*. Ministry of Agriculture, Fisheries and Food, Leaflet 246. (7 pp.)

ANON. (1983). *Fireblight*. Ministry of Agriculture, Fisheries and Food (ADAS), un-numbered leaflet. (4 pp.)

ANON. (1986). *Honey fungus in ornamental plantings*. Forestry Commission Pathology Advisory Service, un-numbered leaflet. (6 pp.)

ANON. (1989). *Pesticides 1989*. Ministry of Agriculture, Fisheries and Food/Health and Safety Executive, Reference Book 500. HMSO. (407 pp.)

ANON. (1989). *Recommendations for tree work*. British Standards Institution, BS 3998.

GARRETT, C.M.E. (1982). *Bacterial canker of cherry and plum*. Ministry of Agriculture, Fisheries and Food, Leaflet 592.

IVENS, G.W. (ed.). (1989). *The UK pesticide guide*. C.A.B. International/British Crop Protection Council. (508 pp.)

PHILLIPS, D.H. AND BURDEKIN, D.A. (1982). *Diseases of forest and ornamental trees*. Macmillan, London and Basingstoke. (435 pp.)

SHIGO, A.L. AND MARX, H.G. (1977). *Compartmentalization of decay in trees*. USDA Forest Service, Agriculture Information Bulletin 405. (73 pp.)

SINCLAIR, W.A., LYON, H.H. AND JOHNSON, W.T. (1987). *Diseases of trees and shrubs*. Comstock Publishing Associates (Ithaca, USA and London, UK). A pictorial guide. (573 pp.)

V Glossary

Ameliorant – Chemicals such as artificial fertilisers and sewage sludge which may be applied to improve soil properties and correct deficiencies.

Anthracnose – A wilt disease of leaves and twigs, principally of London plane.

Apical dominance – Growth concentrated on the leader, which tends to produce a straight stem and conical crown.

Bare root stock – Plants lifted from the nursery soil and despatched to the planting site with their roots bare of soil.

Bridge grafting – Method of grafting young shoots to bridge a girdling wound, usually on a specimen tree's stem.

Callusing – The growth of new tissue across a wound, derived from living cells at the edge; this can protect the tree from fungal and bacterial attack.

Cambium – Cellular tissue beneath a tree's bark, in which the annual growth of wood and bark occurs.

Canker – Dead area of a branch or stem caused by fungal or bacterial attack.

Canopy – The mass of foliage and branches formed collectively by the crowns of trees.

Coppice – Trees felled close to the ground so as to produce shoots from the resulting stools, giving rise to successive crops of poles and sticks cut over a rotation.

Cord – A measure of stacked round timber, comprising a stack 2.4 m × 1.2 m × 1.2 m.

Crown – The leafy canopy of a tree.

Cultivar – A cultivated variety, or sub-division, of a species, consisting of plants which differ in some heritable form from what is regarded as typical of the species; also applied to members of a hybrid group.

Distal – The part of a branch furthest from the point of attachment to the stem.

Epidermis – The outer protective layer of many plant organs, particularly leaves.

Exotics – Tree species which are not indigenous or native.

Feathered – A small tree furnished with lateral shoots.

Fireblight – A disease mainly of the pome fruited group, but also of other Rosaceae, caused by the bacterium *Erwinia amylovora*.

Flush pruning – Removal of branches flush to the stem.

Formative pruning – Pruning a young plant to achieve a desired shape or form.

Girdling or **ring-barking** – Damage to a tree in which bark has been removed from its entire circumference.

Half standard – Plant size of between 1.8 m and 2.1 m height.

Heavy standard – Plant size of between 3.0 m and 3.5 m height.

Honeydew – Sticky exudate produced by aphids, which can cause a nuisance when it drips on to anything beneath an infested tree.

Hoppus measure – Imperial measure of volume used in the timber trade, being replaced by metric measure.

Increment borer – Tool used to extract a core sample from a tree so that annual ring widths can be measured and compared.

Leader – An uppermost shoot on a tree or stem.

Lopping – Term sometimes used to describe the pruning of large branches.

Mulching – The application of a layer of suitable material, e.g. mulch mats, bark, to the soil surface to conserve moisture, reduce soil temperature fluctuations and suppress weed growth around a young tree.

Needle mining – A method of feeding by insects which bore into conifer needles.

Notch planting – Technique of planting whereby tree roots are inserted into a notch formed by cutting and holding open slits which can be straight or 'L' or 'T' shaped.

Occlusion – The closing of a wound by the formation of a callus across it.

Phytotoxic – Any substance harmful to plant tissue and plant growth.

Pit planting – Planting in a pit of prepared or cultivated soil.

Pollarding – The cutting of a young tree's stem (usually above 1 m height) in order to encourage several leaders to develop.

Proximal – The part of a branch nearer to the point of attachment to the stem.

Re-saw – A circular or band saw used to cut sawn timber.

Ring-barking – See 'Girdling'.

Root balled plants – Field grown plants which are lifted with soil attached to the roots and the root ball wrapped with hessian or similar material.

Root collar – The bottom of the stem, usually at ground level.

Root scorch – Damage to roots through direct contact with inorganic fertiliser.

Root:shoot ratio – The ratio of root growth to the aerial part of a plant.

Scion – Shoot of a plant cut for grafting.

Screef – Exposed soil after the organic layer and vegetation from the surface has been removed. (Also used as a verb)

Sets – Woody shoots of species which will root easily when inserted into the soil.

Shake – Timber defect in the form of fissures or splits in the wood of the growing tree.

Stag-headed – Trees with dead branches protruding from the top of a live crown, as a result of old age, injury or other misfortune.

Standard – (1) Individual tree left to grow on to maturity. (2) Plant size of between 2.75 m and 3.0 m height.

Stem cavity – A pocket of decay where the rotted material has disintegrated to cause a cavity.

Storing – Permitting previously coppiced stems to grow on to large size.

Stumping back – Cutting back the stems of young seedling trees to induce the formation of a coppice stool.

Topping – The removal of the crown of a mature or semi-mature tree.

Transplant – Small tree, less than 1.2 m in height, which has been moved from one nursery bed to another to improve root development.

Treeshelter – Plastic tube placed around a newly planted tree to encourage fast early growth and offer some protection from mammals and chemical sprays.

Turf planting – Technique of planting whereby a square of turf is cut out and inverted, and the tree's roots inserted in a notch cut through the inverted turf.

Undercut plants – Small tree whose roots have been severed in order to improve development without transplanting.

Vascular function – The mechanism by which nutrients in solution are conducted within a tree.

Whip – Young tree, between 1.2 m and 2.5 m in height, consisting only of a single slender stem.

Index

(Where headings are followed by a string of references the most important are printed in **bold** type. Table 6.1 (pages 48–62), the tree selection list, which is in alphabetical order, has not been indexed.)

Printed in the United Kingdom for Her Majesty's Stationery Office
Dd0291265 7.89 70C 563064 12521